Praise for
12 Things to Do to Quit Smoking

Heath's book is a valuable resource for the person research-ing quit methods available on the market today. Presented in a neutral way, the information encourages readers to choose the quit aid that works best for them.

—Terry Martin
Guide to About.com Smoking Cessation

T0106645

12 Things to
Do to Quit Smoking

12 Things to Do to Quit Smoking

Heath Dingwell, Ph.D.

TURNER
PUBLISHING COMPANY

"Pain is temporary. Quitting is forever."
~ Anonymous

Turner Publishing Company
www.turnerpublishing.com

12 Things to Do to Quit Smoking

Copyright © 2010 Turner Publishing Company

Library of Congress Cataloging-in-Publication Data

Dingwell, Heath.
 12 things to do to quit smoking / Heath Dingwell.
    p. cm.
 ISBN 978-1-59652-584-9
 1. Smoking cessation. I. Title. II. Title: Twelve things to do to quit smoking.
 HV5740.D56 2010
 616.86'506--dc22

2010004467

"You must do the things you think you cannot do."
~ Eleanor Roosevelt

Contents

Introduction

Introduction

Smoking sucks. It's not the most eloquent way to put it, but it works. If you're a smoker, you probably know that smoking lowers your life expectancy by approximately fourteen years. According to the Centers for Disease Control and Prevention, smoking can be blamed for 90 percent of all lung cancer deaths in men and 80 percent in women. In 2008 it was estimated that over 161,000 lung cancer deaths occurred that year. This means that nearly 91,000 men and 72,000 women died from lung cancer that year alone. To put it in perspective, imagine if some major league and college football stadiums were filled with people and then everyone in them was killed. That's a lot of people.

The CDC says that smoking also causes the following types of cancer: stomach, pancreatic, kidney, bladder, esophageal, larynx, cervical, uterine, oral, and acute myeloid leukemia. Now, I could go on and on about all of the health effects associated with smoking, but I'm sure you get the picture. Smoking does a lot of damage to your body. Not to mention what exposure to secondhand smoke does to the people around you. And it can be prevented.

Maybe that's why you decided to look at this book. You're contemplating quitting. Good for you! Or you're looking to get this for someone who wants to quit. That's great too! Hopefully that person will be appreciative of your concern and desire to help.

This book is a resource. My goal is to share various smoking cessation strategies that have been shown to work. Although I put more faith in certain approaches than others, I recognize that quitting is a very personal experience. What works for you will not work for plenty of other people, and vice versa. That is why so many different strategies are listed. You can read about each one and go with those that make the most sense for you.

Unlike some books or programs designed to "sell" you on a certain approach, this book simply provides you with information. I don't know about you, but I've read books on different topics in which the author tried to advocate his own strategies. Although they may be valid strategies, it makes you wonder what you're not being told. In this book, I've included information that I agree and disagree with. My goal is to offer you knowledge, not attempt to manipulate you into trying one treatment over another. Whenever possible, I've pointed out why I believe certain strategies are better or worse, giving you my research-based opinions as food for thought.

Most of the chapters include presentations of research findings. These aren't meant to bore you. Instead, they are to help you understand the effectiveness of each approach. One thing you'll notice is that the success rate for any given strategy isn't high. Quitting the habit, and staying smoke-free for a long time, is a complex task. And many strategies are not designed with long-term success in mind.

Medications and nicotine replacement therapies do a good job helping people quit, but they don't address the psychological component of nicotine addiction. Smoking becomes second nature, and undoing the habit is a psychological task. Identifying the reasons you smoke requires self-reflection. Finding alternatives to smoking and making them habit takes time.

Going back to the research for a moment, I rarely discuss studies that found an approach to be ineffective. There are many reasons a study may fail to find support for a cessation approach, but that does not mean the strategy truly doesn't work. Other factors involved in the research, such as the people studied, the setting, how success was measured, and so on, can play a huge role. The fact that some studies found positive results is evidence that each approach works to some degree. As I said before, what works for you will not work for plenty of other people.

Most chapters also contain a list of resources to provide you with more information on the material covered. Usually Web sites are listed because they are the quickest way to gather more material. Some chapters don't have this list because there wasn't more information that needed to be added.

In this handy book, you'll find information on nicotine replacement therapies, including nicotine gum, the patch, lozenges, nasal spray, and inhalers. Although nicotine is very addictive, these nicotine replacement therapies work by providing nicotine to your body in a healthier way than smoking. The nicotine patch is the only therapy that provides a steady stream of nicotine to the body. Other therapies deliver the nicotine only when you use them. With the exceptions of the nasal spray and inhaler, you can find these products at most stores and don't need a prescription.

You'll also read about several medications you can try to help you quit. The most effective medication, according to the research, is Chantix. This new medication has been on the market for approximately four years and is the first medication specifically designed for smoking cessation. The most well-known medication for cessation is Zyban, which has been available for more than a decade, although reliable, head-to-head studies with Chantix show that Chantix works for more people. Several other medications have been shown to be effective as well but have not received approval from the U.S. Food and Drug Administration for smoking cessation. However, research has shown they can help, and you'll find plenty of doctors who are willing to prescribe them if other options don't work.

Two chapters are devoted to discussions on treatment centers, support groups, and quitlines. You will find that there are outpatient and inpatient treatment centers around the country. Similar to alcohol and drug rehabilitation facilities, these centers provide structured support for those wishing to stop smoking. You'll learn that support can also be found in every state through a quitline—a telephone, and sometimes Internet, support service.

One section deals with cognitive behavioral therapy, a psychological approach to smoking cessation. Think of cognitive behavioral therapy as a problem-oriented approach: in order to develop healthier coping strategies, you focus on identifying triggers that lead you to smoke. It's not one of those in-depth, talk-about-your childhood approaches to treatment.

The chapter on psychological therapy also describes aversion therapy, a more controversial approach to smoking cessation because it involves punishment. The idea behind this is to equate smoking with a punishment (or negative consequences), which reduces or eliminates the rewards of smoking. Aversion therapy has fallen out of favor with most professionals, but it does work for some smokers.

You'll also find a discussion on quitting cold turkey. This is also a controversial approach because overcoming a nicotine addiction is so difficult. However, there is research that shows quitting cold turkey does work. This approach involves using willpower, a key component to quitting regardless of the method used. Smokers will face obstacles when quitting and trying to remain smoke-free. It takes willpower to overcome obstacles and fight cravings and urges when they return.

Another option discussed in *12 Things* is enrolling in clinical trials for smoking cessation. There are hundreds of clinical trials around the country that are studying the effectiveness of medications, replacement therapies, and other strategies for smoking cessation. Some trials are designed to test new medications, while others conduct further studies on existing ones. Other trials evaluate alternative treatments such as acupuncture. Clinical trials don't cost anything to participate in, and participants are often reimbursed.

Several chapters provide information on natural approaches to smoking cessation, such as diet and exercise, meditation, hypnosis, and acupuncture. This includes discussion on the fascinating strategy of laser acupuncture, which uses low-energy lasers instead of needles, and has produced phenomenal results according to a study that is discussed in this book. Research has also indicated that meditation and hypnosis can be helpful with smoking cessation. These two techniques may also help improve your life overall. Incorporating a healthy diet and exercise routine is good advice in general.

No matter how you approach the smoking cessation process, remember that the information in this book is not a substitute for the advice of medical professionals; rather, it provides practical recommendations to jumpstart your plan. Before implementing the process to quit, you should speak with a doctor, psychiatrist, or other medical professional who can help determine what options are best for you.

By the time you finish the book, you'll have a comprehensive view of potential options for quitting. I hope you find several recommendations worth trying. One suggestion is that prior to implementing a specific technique or therapy discussed in this book, you should develop a short-term and a long-term game plan to increase your chances of long-term success. As more time passes, more people relapse and start smoking again, so developing initial goals can help keep you on track. Please take this into account as you get started. I can't stress enough how much it will prove beneficial.

I hope that what you ultimately decide to try works for you. And thank you for reading this. I appreciate it.

Best wishes,
Heath Dingwell

The 12 Things

~ 1 ~

Develop an action plan

~ 1 ~

Develop an action plan

"It's never too late—in fiction or in life—to revise."
—Nancy Thayer

Are you the type of person who likes to have a plan in place before doing something? Or are you the type who likes to "fly by the seat of your pants?" If you like to have a plan, making one is a vital thing to do to help you quit smoking. If planning isn't your thing, read through this chapter anyway. Even if you start off without a plan, you will likely find that you should have one at some point.

Creating a series of actions and steps then writing them down allows you to take your plan more seriously than you would with just a mental plan. By writing down your plan and goals, you're reinforcing your desire to quit. The act of writing down a goal may not sound like a big deal, but it is. Psychologists, therapists, self-help specialists, and others who counsel people almost always suggest creating a list of goals. Two world-acclaimed motivational speakers, Brian Tracy and Anthony Robbins, also believe we should write out our goals. Anthony Robbins, in his book *Awaken The Giant Within,* devotes a whole chapter to goal-setting and the positive force it creates in helping people make changes in their lives and developing a mindset conducive to success.

As it relates to smoking, ask yourself why you want to quit. List all of the reasons. What changes do you want to see in yourself as you quit smoking? Be as specific as possible. Instead of writing something generic like "I want to be healthy," write, "I want to have more stamina," or "I want my skin to look better," or "I want my lungs to heal." The more detail you provide, the more you'll reinforce what you want to accomplish.

You'll also want to set a "quit date." This is part of the planning process. Selecting a date and then preparing for it reinforces your intent to quit. If you don't set a date and simply decide to quit once you have accomplished everything you need to do so, chances are you'll find yourself procrastinating. You can't start tomorrow because it's your neighbor's cousin's best friend's birthday. And the day after doesn't work because you have to buy a lottery ticket. The day after that might work, but . . . you get the picture. Pick a date and stick with it.

Talk with your doctor before the quit date. You can discuss whether it will be appropriate to use one of the prescription medications designed to help people quit smoking. Your doctor may have other suggestions for you based on your medical background and overall health.

Be sure to inform your friends and family of your decision. Having the support of others can be extremely helpful, especially when you might want to smoke and need a distraction. Plus, some of your friends or family may smoke. Hopefully when you're around they'll refrain from smoking, or at least go somewhere else so you'll be less tempted to light up.

It's also important that you recognize the difficulties and potential relapses when trying to quit smoking. As you may have heard, "It ain't no walk in the park." If it was easy to quit, then more people would do it. But it's not easy. There's a rumor that cigarettes are addicting—turns out that "rumor" is true! In fact, they are designed to be addicting. Nicotine itself is addicting. What's worse is cigarettes also have ammonia and acetaldehyde in them, among other chemicals. Both of these chemicals augment the addictiveness of nicotine. Think of cigarettes as chemically engineered addiction sticks. Remember that when the going gets tough. If you do have problems and relapse, don't beat yourself up. Relax. It happens. It took awhile for you to develop the habit, and it'll take some time to break it.

Another part of your action plan is to identify any triggers that make you want to smoke. Maybe you drink alcohol and always smoke at the same time. Or maybe when you're really stressed out, you reach for the pack. Once you've made that list, see what triggers you can avoid, or find alternative ways to deal with them. Obviously you won't be able to avoid everything, especially if stress is a trigger. Just don't smoke to deal with the stress—it defeats the purpose of quitting!

The last thing you need to do when developing a plan is to get yourself into the proper mindset. This is difficult for almost everyone trying to quit. People relapse. But always remember that you can quit smoking. You can do this.

The United States Public Health Services, part of the U.S. Department of Health and Human Services, provides advice on how to develop an action plan for quitting, which overlaps with the advice

I have discussed here. The action plan is created over a five-day period. First, you should meet with your doctor about your desire to quit smoking. You should also pick a date to quit and then meet with your doctor to discuss your goal. Five days before the quit date, you should list your reasons for wanting to quit. Your friends and family should also be told of your decision. Four days before the quit date, you'll want to start paying attention to your smoking triggers.

Three days before your target date, make a list of the things you can do or buy with the money you'll save by not smoking. You should also identify people you can turn to when you need help—are there any friends, family, or local support groups you can turn to? If you are interested in finding any support groups, call your doctor or local hospital. You can also join the local chapter of the American Lung Association, American Heart Association, or American Cancer Society (all discussed in later chapters).

Two days prior to your quit date, go purchase the cessation aids you plan to use. If you have met with your doctor and are going to use medications to help you quit, make sure you have them filled.

The day before your target date, think about how you'll reward yourself for quitting. Are you going to take a mini-vacation? Buy that new fifty-inch flat-screen TV you've been eyeing? You should also make an appointment to see your dentist. Get your teeth cleaned. At the end of the day, it is recommended that you throw away all of your cigarettes and matches. That includes any secret stashes you've made to "help out" when the going gets tough.

Next is the quit day! Be sure to stay very busy—this will help keep your mind and body distracted (at least somewhat). Try to change any routines or behaviors that you associate with smoking. Remind family and friends that you're in the process of quitting. Treat yourself and go celebrate. Just don't drink!

The rest of the book provides information that you can use when developing your action plan. It is important to remember that your plan is not set in stone. You may need to make changes along the way. Certain products may not work. Or you may need to have your doctor prescribe medication. It's okay to change the plan as long as you focus on the ultimate goal of quitting.

Below are some resources to help begin the quest to stop smoking. Be sure to use the rest of this book to help design your action plan. You'll be thankful for it later!

Resources

There are several resources available to help you develop an action plan and carry it out. These include:

Quitlines. All states have quitlines to help people quit smoking. You can do an Internet search to find the quitline in your state. You can also call the national quitline at 1-800-QUIT-NOW. From here you'll be redirected to the quitline for your state.

American Lung Association. The American Lung Association has a wealth of information on the dangers of smoking. Their Web site, www.lungusa.org, also provides information on ways to quit smoking.

Centers for Disease Control and Prevention. The CDC provides plenty of information on smoking and smoking cessation. Their Web site is www.cdc.gov/tobacco.

American Cancer Society. The ACS is a great resource to learn more about smoking and smoking cessation. Their Web site is www.cancer.org.

Smokefree.gov. The federal government's Web site is dedicated to helping people quit smoking.

~ 2 ~

What you're getting into

— 2 —

What you're getting into

"Quitting smoking is easy. I've done it a thousand times."

—Mark Twain

I know you've heard that kicking the habit is difficult. Repeating this statement isn't meant to get you down. In fact, it's the opposite. If you know what you're up against, then you can better prepare for the journey ahead. And if you do stumble here or there, hopefully you won't be upset with yourself. You want to take control over smoking, not have it continue to control you.

The American Cancer Society has publicly stated that nicotine, a natural substance found in tobacco, is as addictive as cocaine or heroin. That means nicotine is pretty strong stuff. What's worse is that the tobacco companies mix in other chemicals to increase the addictive nature of nicotine.

There are more than 4,000 chemicals found in cigarette smoke, and at least fifty of these are known to cause cancer. As mentioned, many of these chemicals found in cigarettes and cigarette smoke are designed to increase the addictive nature of smoking. For example, research has indicated that the chemical acetaldehyde helps to enhance the effects of nicotine and make cigarettes even more addicting. Ammonia, another chemical found in cigarettes, increases the amount of nicotine produced in tobacco smoke. The more nicotine that is available to a smoker, the more rewarding it is to smoke.

A third chemical that has received attention is levulinic acid. This chemical helps desensitize your upper respiratory tract, meaning that you can inhale more smoke because the acid will lessen the irritation smoke causes to your lungs. It also helps the nicotine attach itself to the chemicals in your brain that give you pleasurable sensation, thus increasing the pleasure of smoking.

Even cocoa is used in cigarettes to increase their addictiveness. The tobacco industry says it helps improve the flavor associated with smoking, but critics disagree. Actually, cocoa contains a chemical called theobromine that helps to open up your airways, allowing you to take deeper breaths. Deeper puffs mean you'll inhale more smoke, which increases the amount of nicotine your body receives. See where this is going?

There are other chemicals in cigarettes that help to mask the irritating effects of smoking. Take menthol, for example. It helps provide a cooling sensation when smoking. It also helps to numb the throat, making it easier to handle the smoke. The easier it is to handle the smoke, the more a person will smoke. The more a person smokes, the more nicotine they absorb, and the more addictive smoking becomes.

A whole book can be written on the additives found in cigarettes. All additives have a purpose, which, generally speaking, is to make smoking more rewarding and enjoyable. This, in turn, makes it more difficult to quit.

Understanding withdrawal symptoms

Setting aside the addictiveness of cigarettes for a moment, another aspect that makes quitting so hard is the withdrawal symptoms. The body becomes used to the presence of nicotine and other chemicals in cigarettes. These chemicals change, to some degree, how the body functions. Just as an alcoholic's body compensates for the presence of alcohol so that the person can function, the same thing happens for smokers. A smoker's body has adjusted and continues to function even with all of the poisons from smoking. Stop smoking and the body has to readjust. This readjustment isn't pleasant and can be downright excruciating for many.

Nicotine lasts in the body for approximately forty-eight hours. According to the American Cancer Society, smokers can start feeling the withdrawal effects even after a few hours without a cigarette. The withdrawal symptoms are the most intense after two to three days, and symptoms can remain for several weeks. Not a fun experience. We don't like to experience pain, and the withdrawal effects cause pain. That's part of the reason it is so hard to quit.

You may experience any of the following withdrawal symptoms:

1. Dizziness
2. Fatigue
3. Headaches
4. Depression
5. Anxiety

6 .Frustration, anger, or impatience
7. Restlessness
8. Irritability
9. Insomnia
10. Nightmares or bad dreams
11. Difficulty concentrating
12. Tight chest
13. Increased appetite
14. Nausea
15. Sore throat and mouth
16. Cravings

On the bright side, these symptoms are at their worst during the first couple of days. Just remember, the symptoms are temporary. That doesn't change the fact that going through withdrawal just down-right stinks. And symptoms are worse for those who smoke more. If you experience symptoms other than those listed here, you should check with your doctor to make sure something else isn't going on.

Some interesting research was published in 2009 about withdrawal symptoms. Doctors wanted to see whether the severity of symptoms varied according to the time of day. Their findings confirmed their hypothesis that withdrawal symptoms were different throughout the day. In particular, cravings were lower in the afternoon, higher in the morning, and highest in the evening. This finding also applied to people who were still smoking. Even people on a nicotine patch showed a similar pattern of cravings. The same pattern also held for overall withdrawal symptoms, such as difficulty concentrating, restlessness and impatience, irritability, and anxiety.

If you notice your withdrawal symptoms follow a similar pattern, please remember this happens to a lot of people who quit smoking. Don't be surprised if you find yourself using more nicotine gum or lozenges during these times (assuming you use these products to help you quit).

Resources

American Cancer Society. www.cancer.org. The ACS is an excellent resource for information on anything related to cancer, include smoking.

American Legacy Foundation. www.americanlegacy.org. This organization is dedicated to educating the public about smoking and its dangerous effects. They created the "truth" smoking prevention campaign.

National Cancer Institute. www.cancer.gov. The institute is part of the U.S. National Institutes of Health. You can speak online with one of their smoking cessation specialists for questions or more information.

Tobacco Wiki. www.tobaccowiki.org. This Web site is an information center on smoking, tobacco, and the tobacco industry. If you are interested in reading tobacco-industry documents that have been made available to the public, you'll find this Web site especially useful.

~ 3 ~

Quitting cold turkey

— 3 —

Quitting cold turkey

"The best way to stop smoking is to just stop—no ifs, ands, or butts."

—*Edith Zittler*

One way to quit smoking is to go "cold tur-key"—just up and quit. If you do an Internet search for quitting cold turkey, you'll find several Web sites that advocate the approach. Whether or not it's a good approach is debatable. According to the National Cancer Institute, less than 5 percent of smokers can quit cold turkey. It will work for some people and not work for many more.

I know someone who smoked for decades and just up and quit one day. That was the end of it. It was hard to tell whether that person suffered from withdrawal effects—he was a naturally cranky person. If the withdrawal was getting to him, no one could tell!

On the other hand, I know people who have made repeated attempts and couldn't quit without incorporating other approaches. The reason is rather simple: some people cannot handle the withdrawal symptoms or subsequent cravings.

If you read enough Web sites, you'll see the definition of "cold turkey" is not consistent. Some people view "cold turkey" as quitting without using any therapies, aids, or medications—not necessarily abruptly stopping. To some, quitting cold turkey means gradually reducing the number of cigarettes smoked until one day the smoker just stops. Most people, however, define "cold turkey" as simply quitting, throwing everything away, and not smoking again. Chances are that's what you think when you hear the term. When I use the phrase, it will refer to abruptly quitting.

There's been research conducted on the effectiveness of quitting cold turkey. In 2007, several doctors published a study that compared the effectiveness of quitting cold turkey versus gradually reducing cigarette smoking. The results were somewhat surprising. The doctors discovered that quitting cold turkey was more successful than gradually quitting. Approximately 10 percent more people (22 percent versus 12 percent) were able to quit cold turkey compared to the gradual approach.

There are a few factors that can influence the success of the cold-turkey approach. They include:

1. How long you've smoked.
2. The number of packs you smoke.
3. Your willpower.
4. Your motivation to quit.
5. Prior attempts to quit. What seemed to work and for how long?

If you are going to quit cold turkey, I definitely recommend reading the sections in the book on aversion therapy, meditation and visualization, and hypnosis. None of the approaches described in those chapters call for the use of nicotine replacement therapy or medications. The techniques can help manage both the withdrawal effects and cravings you'll experience.

Another suggestion is to buy some lollipops, gum, or Tootsie Rolls. Keep your mouth busy. Your dentist may not agree with that approach, unless you go with sugar-free items. Oh well, you can't please everyone. Just be sure to floss and brush your teeth at least a couple of times a day. Another suggestion is to do an Internet search on quitting cold turkey. You'll find plenty of tips, along with success and failure stories.

Every year the American Cancer Society holds the Great American Smokeout. This annual event started in 1977 (some states had their own smoke-outs before then) and occurs on the third Thursday of November. The event challenges people to quit smoking for a day. The Smokeout does not promote the cold-turkey method, although people are encouraged to stop for just a day. Hopefully this will help motivate some to quit permanently. For those who will attempt to quit smoking, the ACS does recommend the use of replacement therapies and medications.

One benefit of going cold turkey is saving money. You don't need money to buy medications or nicotine replacement therapies. You don't even need to buy candy if you don't want to.

Resources

WhyQuit.com. Billed as the "The Internet's leading cold turkey quit smoking resource." If you are going to try cold turkey, take a look at this informative site.

~ 4 ~

Nicotine replacement therapy

— 4 —

Nicotine replacement therapy

"Fortunately, there's more than one way to quit smoking . . . the catch is you must choose wisely to become smoke-free."

—*Arthur A. Hawkins II*

Many professionals believe that nicotine replacement therapies (NRT) have revolutionized the way to quit smoking. Nicotine replacement therapies are popular because they are designed to help minimize the withdrawal symptoms associated with quitting. Some replacement therapies smokers can choose from include gum, patches, nasal spray, inhalants, and lozenges.

If you decide to use one of these aids, you should talk with your doctor first. Even though you can buy gum, patches, and lozenges without a prescription, you are using a medication. As with most medications, there are side effects and drug interactions to take into account.

Nicotine gum

Nicotine gum has been on the market for over twenty years. You can purchase the gum at pharmacies, grocery stores, department stores, and even at many gas station convenience stores. You can also search the Internet to find online stores that sell it.

The gum comes in two strengths, 2 mg and 4 mg. The lower dose is for those who smoke no more than twenty-four cigarettes a day. The higher dose is for smokers who smoke at least twenty-five cigarettes a day. You should only use approximately ten pieces of gum a day, although the maximum number of pieces is thirty. Read the instructions on the box, and talk to your pharmacist and doctor to see what they recommend. It is also important that you avoid coffee and tea, wine, carbonated drinks, beer, fruit juices, and acidic drinks for fifteen minutes before and after chewing the gum. These drinks can block the absorption of the gum's nicotine. That means you'll be chewing an expensive piece of gum that has no benefit.

Studies have shown the gum does help with smoking cessation. A study published in 2009 examined the effectiveness of using nicotine gum as part of gradually reducing smoking. People started using the gum as they decreased the number of cigarettes they smoked until they stopped smoking. The results indicated that those using the gum were approximately three times more likely than those using a placebo gum to be smoke-free twenty-eight days after quitting. At the six-month mark, those who used the nicotine gum were still nearly three times more likely to be smoke-free than those who had used the placebo. The nicotine gum definitely helped with cessation.

There are different brands of nicotine gum. The name brands include Nicorette, Nicotrol, and Habitrol. However, as with most prescription medications, you can also find generics. Go into any pharmacy or department store chain and chances are that company will have its own brand of nicotine gum. For example, Rite Aid, Walgreens and Target sell their own nicotine gums. Go with the brand name or generic? Your call.

Nicorette gum comes in various flavors: original, mint, fresh mint, fruit chill, cinnamon surge, and white ice mint. Even if you're not a fan of different flavors, you have to admit any of these will most likely taste better than a cigarette.

Nicotine gum is designed to be chewed differently than regular gum. Pop a piece in your mouth and chew on it a few times. Break it down so it's not hard. Once you notice your mouth tingling or a peppery taste, place it between your gum and cheek and leave it there. The nicotine from the gum will be absorbed into your system. You can occasionally chew it and put it back between the cheek and gum. After thirty minutes, it's time to throw it away.

The goal of nicotine gum is to allow your body to continue to receive nicotine without smoking. You gradually decrease the amount of gum you use until you can stop using it. Quitting will still require willpower and planning on your part. Also, nicotine gum can be addictive. A study published in 2009 found that 83 percent of people who used the gum for at least three months said they used it because it's addicting. Only 42 percent indicated one of the reasons they use it is to help avoid smoking relapses. However, it's better to be addicted to the nicotine gum than to cigarettes. The gum is not chemically enhanced to increase its addictiveness. Plus, there's no smoke, so it'll be easier on your body.

Nicotine gum can also be used to help fight cravings once you've quit smoking and stopped using the gum on a regular basis. There will be times you crave a cigarette. And there will be times the craving wins. Keep some gum handy and use that when a craving gets too strong.

According to both the U.S. National Library of Medicine and the National Institutes of Health, you can use a few strategies to reduce the amount of gum you use over time. One idea is to reduce the number of pieces you chew by one every four to seven days. Another option is to shorten the length of time you use each piece of gum. Instead of going the full thirty minutes, see how you do with the gum for ten to fifteen minutes. If you can reduce the chewing time for four to seven days, then start decreasing the number of pieces you chew as well.

Another idea is to substitute regular gum for some of the nicotine gum. Start small and then replace more nicotine gum with regular gum over time. Of course, it is recommended that you use sugarfree gum. After all, you don't want to get any cavities.

There are side effects associated with nicotine gum. Don't be surprised if you get headaches or an upset stomach, if you feel dizzy, or if your jaw aches. Nicotine gum takes more effort to chew than regular gum, so your jaw muscles will get a workout. Also, you could develop ulcers in your mouth. You may want to give your dentist a call for suggestions to minimize any mouth irritations.

If you have breathing difficulties, seizures, or an abnormal heartbeat, get to the local hospital immediately to be checked out. Most directions will tell you to immediately notify your doctor if you have any of these symptoms. However, in all likelihood, you'll be told to go the hospital for an evaluation. You can let your doctor know later how everything turned out. Of course, your doctor will know you've been using nicotine gum. After all, you did discuss it with her before you started. Right?

Nicotine patch

"Nicotine patches are great. Stick one over each eye and you can't find your cigarettes."—Anonymous

The nicotine patch is the second-most-popular nicotine replacement therapy. As you probably know, the nicotine patch is a skin patch. Just stick it on your body somewhere and leave it alone for sixteen to twenty-four hours. The patch is probably the easiest replacement therapy to use because you change it once a day. In the words of inventor Ron Popeil, you "set it and forget it."

The patch can take awhile to work. The nicotine in the patch has to pass through the skin and into the bloodstream, which can take up to three hours. Just don't use this delay as an excuse to smoke for a couple of hours.

Unlike nicotine gum or lozenges, the patch is not to be used when cravings strike. It is designed to provide the body with a steady stream of nicotine. Hopefully, the patch reduces the number of cravings and their intensity. However, you can also use nicotine gum or lozenges to help with the cravings. You'll definitely want to talk with a pharmacist or doctor before doing that so you can know how many pieces of gum you can chew while wearing it.

The side effects of the patch are similar to those of the nicotine gum. They include dizziness, headache, diarrhea, vomiting, and upset stomach. It is also possible that there will be redness or swelling around the site of the patch. The severe, go-to-the-hospital side effects include seizures, difficulty breathing, abnormal heartbeat, and severe rash or swelling. If you are taking other medications, you should ask your doctor about potential drug interactions.

A two-step or three-step process is involved when using the patch, depending on how much you smoke. A two-step approach is suggested for those who smoke less than ten cigarettes a day, while the three-step approach is for those who smoke more than ten a day. Step one consists of wearing a 21 mg nicotine patch for six weeks. The second step involves wearing a 14 mg patch for two weeks. The last step involves wearing a 7 mg patch for another two weeks. After that, the patch is no longer worn. Those who only need the two-step process should follow steps two and three.

A review of medical research shows that the patch does help with smoking cessation. Research from 2008 found that when smokers start wearing the patch before they quit, they are more likely to succeed once they've stopped smoking. Using the patch improved the chances of quitting, and starting the patch before the official quit date proved to be more effective than starting it on the quit date.

On average, using the patch almost doubles the chances of quitting. However, the percentage of people who successfully quit by only using the patch is still low. For example, one study found that almost 88 percent of smokers were initially able to stop smoking when using the patch. That sounds fantastic! However, after one week, that number dropped to 40 percent—less than half the people in the study were able to hold out for a week. After eight weeks, almost 45 percent were smoke-free. However, at the end of six months, slightly more than 34 percent of the participants were still smoke-free.

Is that a success? It obviously depends on your perspective. Long-term success with only the patch is low, but that doesn't mean the patch is useless. Far from it! What it should tell you is it takes much more than one nicotine replacement therapy to achieve long-term success. Research shows that combining the patch with other nicotine replacement therapies, such as the gum or lozenge, will further increase your chances of success. A study that came out in late 2009 compared the effectiveness of the various replacement therapies and the medication bupropion. The most effective approach was using the patch and the lozenge together. At the end of six months, approximately 40 percent of participants using this method were still smoke-free. Unfortunately, the authors of this study did not examine the effectiveness of nicotine gum. Because the gum and lozenge work on the same principle—use them when you need to—it would be interesting to see if the patch and gum worked as well, or better, than the patch and lozenge.

As previously mentioned, the patch provides a steady stream of nicotine to the body. If you use only the patch, you'll have to rely on willpower to deal with any cravings that strike. However, as you read the remaining chapters, you'll notice that the percentage of smokers who successfully quit using prescription medications and other methods is not much higher than those who opt for the patch alone.

Nicotine lozenges

The third over-the-counter nicotine replacement therapy is the nicotine lozenge. The lozenge is similar to the gum: you put it in your mouth and essentially leave it alone. It takes between twenty and thirty minutes for the lozenge to dissolve. There's no chewing, and definitely no swallowing—unless, of course, you love nausea and wicked stomachaches.

The lozenge comes in two strengths, 2 mg and 4 mg. As with the other replacement therapies, the higher dose is for heavier smokers. If you decide to quit by using the lozenge, you should follow a twelve-week plan. For the first six weeks, use a lozenge every hour or two. For the next three weeks, use one every two to four hours. During the last three weeks, use a lozenge every four to eight hours, and after twelve weeks, stop using them altogether.

There are fewer side effects with the lozenge as compared to the patch and gum. Heartburn and sore throat are the most common side effects. Don't be surprised if your mouth is sore or irritated for a while. Once again, if you experience an irregular heartbeat, take a trip to the hospital.

As with the other replacement therapies, research has shown that the lozenge is an effective aid for smoking cessation. A 2009 study found that after using lozenges for one week, 29 percent of people had not started smoking again. This jumped to almost 41 percent after eight weeks, but dropped to 33 percent after six months. Another study looked at the effectiveness of the lozenge in dealing with various withdrawal and craving symptoms. Although the authors did not report on the smoking abstinent rates, they did report that the lozenge significantly helped with mood, concentration, memory, and attention.

Nicotine nasal spray and inhaler

"People who have never had an addiction don't understand how hard it can be."—Payne Stewart

The last two nicotine replacement therapies discussed here are the nasal spray and inhaler. Much of the information about these two therapies has already been mentioned in prior sections.

If you're interested in the nasal spray or inhaler, you will need to talk with your doctor because neither is available over the counter. Because these are prescription medications, your health insurance may cover them. Call the insurance company before filling the prescription to make sure it's covered. Your doctor may already know—chances are you're not the first person to want one of these therapies.

At this point you can probably guess some of the side effects of the nasal spray. Because the nicotine is being administered through a nasal spray, your nose, mouth, and throat may become irritated. Your eyes may water and you may have a runny nose. The thought of liquid nicotine running out of the nose isn't very attractive, so be sure to keep some tissues handy. The irritation can also cause you to sneeze and cough—once again, keep the tissues nearby. It's best not to swallow or drink the nasal spray. If that happens, you'll want to immediately talk with the nice folks at the poison control center to see what you should do next.

Research has shown that both the inhaler and nasal spray are effective in helping people quit smoking. A study published in 1996 found that the nicotine inhaler has short-term effects on smoking abstinence. Participants were allowed to use the inhaler between four and twenty times a day for a period of three months. Between the third and sixth month, participants had to start using the inhaler less, finally stopping at the end of the sixth month. After one week of treatment, 46 percent of people using the inhaler were abstinent. This figure dropped to 24 percent at the end of three months, 17 percent after six months, and 13 percent after one year.

Similar results were found in a study published in 2000. In that study, the researchers compared the effectiveness of the inhaler alone versus using the inhaler and a nicotine patch. Once again, people used the inhaler as needed for three months and then tapered off usage. After six months, 22 percent of people who used the inhaler alone were still abstinent. This figure dropped to 14 percent after one year. The group who also received the nicotine patch did not fare much better. After six months, 25 percent of that group were still abstinent, while almost 20 percent were still abstinent at the one-year mark.

However, the nicotine patch was administered for only the first six weeks, which is not that long.

One study compared the effectiveness of the inhaler to the nasal spray. The results were similar for the inhaler and nasal spray groups. Approximately 24 percent of each group had completely refrained from smoking for twelve weeks while using the replacement therapies. Unfortunately, no follow-up data was collected, so it was not possible to determine the percentage of participants abstinent at six months and one year.

One possible downside to the nasal spray and inhaler is being embarrassed by using either in public. Neither is as discrete as a patch, gum, or lozenge. Although it is not a big deal to be seen with an inhaler or nasal spray, some people may be hesitant to use these products. Obviously, not using them is no problem since there are other options available.

Resources

Nicorette.com. Nicorette is made by GlaxoSmith-Kline. Their Web site has useful information on Nicorette, nicotine addiction, and smoking cessation. The company also offers a rewards program for earning coupons and gifts as you continue to use their product.

Nicotrol.com. The Web site for the Nicotrol brand of nicotine gum.

Drugstore.com. One of the leaders in online shopping for health and wellness products. Although plenty of online stores offer smoking cessation products, I've ordered items from drugstore.com in the past and never had a problem.

NicodermCQ.com. The Web site for GlaxoSmith-Kline's nicotine patch.

Commitlozenge.com. The Web site has a similar design as the one for Nicorette gum because both are made by GlaxoSmithKline. The smoking information is the same, except this site has information about the lozenge.

– 5 –

Prescription medications

− 5 −

Prescription medications

"Expensive medicines are always good—if not for the patient, at least for the druggist."
—*Russian proverb*

Another way to help you quit smoking is to use prescription medications. A couple of medications are used solely for smoking cessation. Then there are other medications that can be taken to help smokers quit but are primarily used to treat other conditions. Using them for smoking cessation is considered "off label," since the U.S. Food and Drug Administration approved them for other conditions.

In order to use a prescription medication, you will need to work with a doctor to discuss the different options available and determine which one you should try first. I say "try first" because one medication may not do the trick. You may have to switch to another one or a combination, or use a medication along with a nicotine replacement therapy.

You've heard that side effects can occur when using a nicotine replacement therapy. The same thing can happen when using prescription medications. A medication may work great in helping you stop smoking; however, if the side effects are severe enough, you'll have to switch medications. Don't worry if that happens. As you'll see, you do have some options to choose from.

Zyban (bupropion)

One of the better-known medications used to help with smoking cessation is Zyban, developed by GlaxoSmithKline. You also may have heard of using Wellbutrin. Zyban and Wellbutrin are the same medication, known as bupropion. The company marketed Zyban for smoking cessation, while Wellbutrin was marketed for depression. Although they are the same medication (bupropion), if a doctor prescribes Wellbutrin, it is considered an off-label use.

There are different forms of bupropion. Some are sustained release, which makes the medication last longer in the body. Other forms are absorbed and metabolized quicker. The sustained release is the most effective option for smoking cessation. Zyban comes in different doses, 100 mg, 150 mg, and 300 mg. Your doctor will determine which strength is best suited for you.

Zyban contains no nicotine and is not designed to be a nicotine replacement therapy. Zyban works by blocking chemicals in the brain that reinforce the effects of nicotine, which means that smoking does not have the same rewarding feel to it. Zyban can be used in conjunction with nicotine replacement therapies. In fact, it's a good idea. When you use more than one approach to quit, you increase your chances of success.

If you are worried about gaining weight as you stop smoking, you may want to consider using Zyban. One of its side effects is weight loss. I don't know too many people who are opposed to losing weight when taking a medication.

As with almost all medications, there are numerous potential side effects with Zyban. These include flushing, increased urination, nervousness and restlessness, nausea, stomach pain, increased sweating, and taste changes. Potentially severe side effects may include allergic reactions, confusion, dark urine, chest pain, fainting, irregular heartbeat, and skin that peels or becomes red, swollen, or blistered. Other symptoms may include severe headache or dizziness, tremors, vision changes, swelling of the mouth, severe joint or muscle pain, severe vomiting or nausea or stomach pain, shortness of breath, unusual swelling, yellowing of the eyes or skin, and worsening depression. If any of these occur, you should immediately call your doctor or go to the hospital.

Bupropion is an antidepressant, so don't be surprised if your doctor or pharmacist mentions the possibility of changes in behavior or having thoughts about suicide. Some research has shown that taking antidepressants increases the possibility of having suicidal thoughts. This does not mean it will happen to you or that taking the medication will make you commit suicide. The research on the relationship between taking antidepressants and committing suicide is considered questionable by some doctors. After discussing with your doctor any concerns you have, do what you're most comfortable with.

After reading this you're probably wondering if you should go near any form of bupropion! The medication is safe—if it wasn't, the Food and Drug Administration would have pulled it off the shelves. These are side effects that can *possibly* occur. You may experience no side effects, a few, or several. If the latter occurs, then you and your doctor could discuss changing medications.

Treatment using bupropion is supposed to last between seven and twelve weeks. This can be extended up to a year, or possibly longer, to help prevent you from starting up the habit again. Bupropion is safe for long-term use, and people who take it for anxiety or depression disorders can stay on it for years.

Over a decade of research indicates bupropion is an effective tool to help people quit smoking. The *New England Journal of Medicine* published a study back in 1999 that compared the effectiveness of bupropion against the nicotine patch. Patients were given one of the following: bupropion, a patch, bupropion plus the patch, or placebo medication. Treatment lasted for nine weeks, and patients were questioned about their smoking behavior at the six- and twelve-month marks. Approximately 35 percent of patients who used bupropion were smoke-free at six months, while only 21 percent of those who used the patch were still abstinent. However, nearly 39 percent of people who used the patch and bupropion were no longer smoking. Only 19 percent of people who took the placebo medication managed to abstain from smoking. At the end of the year, the percentage of those who remained abstinent dropped: 35 percent for those who used the patch and medication, 30 percent for those who used bupropion, and 16 percent who used only the patch.

An interesting study came out in 2001 that indicated long-term use of bupropion can be beneficial in helping people remain smoke-free. Patients were given bupropion for seven weeks. Those who remained abstinent through the seven weeks were then divided into two groups: one group continued to receive bupropion for another forty-five weeks, and the other received a placebo pill. At the end of the forty-five weeks, approximately 55 percent of those still taking bupropion had not relapsed. Slightly more than 42 percent of people taking the placebo also had not started smoking again. Six months later, at the seventy-eight-week mark, almost 48 percent of the bupropion group and 38 percent of the placebo group were smoke-free.

There was one more interesting finding in this study. It took over twice as long for people to re-lapse if they were on bupropion compared to the placebo pill (the median relapse time was 156 days compared to 65 days). Another benefit of taking bupropion proved to be weight loss. Those taking the medication gained significantly less weight than those on the placebo pill.

Overall, bupropion is a good medication to try for smoking cessation. The research indicates that it is an effective medication and can be used for long periods of time. The side effects can be problematic for some people, but that's to be expected.

Chantix (varenicline)

"If your body's not right, the rest of your day will go all wrong. Take care of yourself."—V. L. Allineare

The "golden child" of smoking-cessation drugs is Chantix. This is the newest prescription medication for smoking cessation and is made by Pfizer. It was approved for smoking cessation by the Food and Drug Administration in 2006.

You can still smoke while taking varenicline, but it's preferable that you don't. However, if you do, you'll experience a decline in the satisfaction you get from smoking. The less rewarding smoking becomes, the more likely you'll stop. The medication also helps to suppress both cravings and withdrawal symptoms. That's what makes this such a good drug to try. Smoking becomes less enjoyable while cravings and withdrawal symptoms are suppressed.

Compared to bupropion and nicotine replacement therapies, there is not as much research on varenicline. This is nothing more than a byproduct of time—the longer varenicline is on the market, the more research will be conducted on its effectiveness. However, the research to date has been promising.

Studies have shown that varenicline is more effective than bupropion and placebos. One study found that 50 percent of people on varenicline and

36 percent of people on bupropion SR indicated they were not smoking (as measured by not having a cigarette in at least a week). This was after being on the medication for twelve weeks. Another study found that 44 percent of people on varenicline versus 30 percent of people on bupropion were not smoking at the end of a twelve-week period. Yet another study found that almost 37 percent of people on varenicline were not smoking after fifty-two weeks. This compares to almost 8 percent of people who were taking the placebo pill.

You may recall the study in the bupropion section in which approximately 55 percent of those on bupropion for a year managed to stay smoke-free at the end of the year. As of this writing, there are no published studies in which patients were treated with varenicline for a total of fifty-two weeks. Several studies have been published in which patients were treated with varenicline for up to twenty-four weeks only.

One study found that at the end of twenty-four weeks of treatment, almost 71 percent of people on varenicline were still smoke-free. Almost 50 percent of those in the placebo group were still smoke-free. At the one-year mark, almost 44 percent who had been on varenicline were still abstaining from smoking, compared to nearly 37 percent who were on the placebo.

Short-term treatment with varenicline does not produce the same level of results as long-term treatment produces. A study in which patients received varenicline for only six weeks had more dismal results after one year. Almost 15 percent of people who took varenicline were still not smoking after the year. This compares to approximately 6 percent who took bupropion and 5 percent who had taken the placebo pill.

Varenicline can also help with your mood while you quit smoking. One study found that it helped with positive mood and reduced negative mood. It also helped people with their memory and ability to pay attention.

The most common side effect of varenicline is nausea. Others include headaches, insomnia, abnormal dreams, gas and constipation, vomiting and retching, change in appetite, and changes in taste. A 2009 research study found that 17 percent of people taking varenicline had to discontinue the medication because of side effects. A 2006 study, however, found that only 9 percent of people had to discontinue varenicline because of side effects.

The U.S. Food and Drug Administration issued a "black-box" warning on varenicline in 2008. There were concerns that the drug caused mood changes and made any existing psychiatric disorders worse. As with bupropion, if you see a doctor for anxiety, depression, or other psychiatric symptoms, you'll want to discuss whether you should try Chantix.

There are other medications your doctor can prescribe if varenicline or bupropion don't work for you. These include nortriptyline, clonidine, gabapentin, and fluoxetine.

Nortriptyline

Nortriptyline, which has a brand name of Pamelor, is another antidepressant that can be used for smoking cessation. This is an older antidepressant known as a tricyclic antidepressant. Research on why nortriptyline helps with smoking cessation is pretty sparse. The exact reasons it works for people trying to quit are unknown, but there are a couple of theories. Because it is an antidepressant, it helps with the depression people may experience when quitting. If you remember, nicotine also acts as an antidepressant. If people start smoking again to help with the depression, then an antidepressant such as nortriptyline can replace the cigarettes.

Some research has shown that taking nortriptyline doubles the rate of abstinence from smoking. One study showed that the one-year abstinence rate for people on the medication was 24 percent. This compares to only 12 percent of those taking a placebo pill. Another study found that almost 21 percent of people on nortriptyline were smoke-free after six months.

The side effects associated with nortriptyline will sound familiar. Increased sweating, mild rash, weight change, diarrhea or constipation, nausea, dry mouth, stomach pain and loss of appetite, numbness or tingling, headache, and blurry vision are the less serious side effects. More serious side effects include mood changes, tremors, chest pain or heaviness, confusion, changes in heart rate (uneven, fast, pounding), and sudden numbness or weakness.

Clonidine

Clonidine, which is marketed as Catapres, is a medication used to treat hypertension. It has also been shown to help with chronic pain, opiate- and alcohol-abuse withdrawal symptoms, and smoking withdrawal symptoms. Compared to nicotine replacement therapies and other medications for smoking cessation, there's been very little research done on the effectiveness of clonidine, with most from the late 1980s through 1990s. Clonidine is believed to work for smoking cessation because it helps counteract some nicotine withdrawal symptoms, including restlessness, tension, irritability, anxiety, and cravings. These symptoms are common in both drug and alcohol withdrawal, so it makes sense that clonidine can help with smoking cessation.

Research shows that clonidine is somewhat effective as a second-line medication (not the first choice of medication for treatment). One study looked at the effectiveness of clonidine after patients had been taking it for twenty-four weeks. Slightly more than 19 percent had been abstinent for the twenty-four weeks. The study also assessed the effectiveness of nicotine gum; almost 37 percent of patients in this group remained smoke-free for the twenty-four weeks. Although clonidine was shown to be effective, it was only half as successful as the gum.

Another study revealed some interesting findings regarding clonidine's effectiveness for men versus women. Clonidine was administered for ten weeks, then patients provided blood samples to determine whether they had stopped smoking. The results indicated that clonidine was not an effective smoking-cessation medication for men. However, it was found to be effective for women, especially those who were most addicted. Women with serious nicotine addiction were 8.5 times more likely to stop smoking when using clonidine compared to those who were on a placebo. It's not well understood why clonidine worked better for women in this study, so more studies would need to be done to see if there is in fact a gender differentiation.

It may not be surprising to learn that there are possible side effects when taking clonidine. The less serious ones include dry mouth, headaches, insomnia, mild skin rash, itching, nausea, vomiting, constipation, loss of appetite, dizziness, drowsiness, nervousness, and a decreased sex drive. You'll want to go straight to the hospital if you have difficulty breathing; if your face, lips, tongue, or throat swells;

or you develop hives. If you start to experience a pounding heartbeat, a very slow heart rate, confusion or hallucinations, shortness of breath, or inability to urinate, it is strongly recommended that you call your doctor. Chances are you'll need to switch medications.

Gabapentin

Gabapentin is marketed under the name Neurontin and is used to treat epilepsy and pain. There is some evidence that it can also help with smoking cessation. However, as with the other drugs discussed in this chapter, more evidence is needed.

An article was published in 2007 by several doctors who looked at the effectiveness of gabapentin for smoking cessation. At the end of the eight-week trial, 28 percent of participants had abstained from all smoking for at least one week. Approximately 24 percent of participants had been smoke-free for at least two weeks. At the six-month mark, 20 percent indicated they had not smoked for at least one week prior to the follow-up survey, and 16 percent had not smoked for at least two weeks. However, doctors who published an article in 2008 reviewed evidence of gabapentin's effectivity and concluded that it did not help with smoking cessation.

Most people have no problems with gabapentin, but as always, there is a chance of experiencing side effects. The most common side effects of gabapentin are dizziness and somnolence (drowsiness). Diarrhea, asthenia (weakness), dry mouth, constipation, and headaches are other side effects. If you use this medication and other symptoms arise, call your doctor to see whether they are a result of the gabapentin.

Gabapentin may be considered a second-line or third-line approach when other medications fail, but at this time, there is a need for more research.

Fluoxetine

Fluoxetine, better known as Prozac, is another antidepressant that has been evaluated for smoking cessation. Fluoxetine was one of the first medications in a class of antidepressants known as selective serotonin reuptake inhibitors. In layman's terms, these help ensure there is more serotonin in the brain, which influences a positive mood. Serotonin is one of the key chemicals in the brain related to mood disorders such as anxiety and depression.

Fluoxetine was approved by the U.S. Food and Drug Administration in 1987 for treating depression. It is not an FDA-approved medication for smoking cessation. However, like many other medications, it is used off-label to treat various conditions, including smoking addictions.

Research results are mixed on its effectiveness for smoking cessation. One of the more rigorous studies found that it did not help more than the placebo medication. The results showed that 43.1

percent of people taking 20 mg of fluoxetine had abstained from smoking, while 35.4 percent of those taking a placebo medication had abstained. Although the results were not significantly different from each other, the 43.1 percent abstinence rate is similar to the success of other medications. Because it can take several weeks for fluoxetine to start working, patients in this group started the medication four weeks before the scheduled quit date and continued taking it for ten weeks after the quit date.

Another study found that fluoxetine initially helped with smoking cessation, but then increased the odds that people would start smoking again. At the six-month mark, those who had been treated with fluoxetine were more than three times as likely to be smoking again, compared to those who took a placebo medication.

The reason fluoxetine may help with smoking cessation is that it helps lessen withdrawal effects, particularly those related to mood. There is no evidence that fluoxetine interferes with the pleasure someone gets from smoking (unlike varenicline, which reduces the pleasure).

There is a great deal of research on smoking and depression, which often go hand-in-hand. If you think you are depressed, talk to your doctor about it. Remember, mood is such an important part of being able to quit. An antidepressant such as fluoxetine can be used long-term to help regulate your mood. If it can increase your chances for successfully quitting, why not explore the possibility? Your doctor should determine what combination of medications you may be able to take. There are more than thirty different antidepressants on the market, with other medications available to help boost the antidepressant effects.

Conclusion

When you read this chapter, there is a chance you may become discouraged because of all the side effects and relative lack of research. Please remember a couple of things. First, all medications have side effects. These medications are safe, but they can effect people differently. If you take a medication that doesn't work well for you, your doctor can recommend another.

Second, there is some evidence that these medications work to help people stop smoking. Even if the evidence for their effectiveness isn't overwhelming, that doesn't mean they can't benefit you. It doesn't matter whether they don't work for other people—what matters is whether they can work for you. Of course, your doctor has to be on board with the idea.

Third, medications such as antidepressants can indirectly help you quit smoking. They may not be designed to interfere with the pleasure you receive when smoking. However, given their impact on mood, they can help provide you with the mental and psychological strength needed to quit for good.

Resources

Drugs.com. The Web site has plenty of information on all of the medications listed in this section. Quality information on bupropion can be accessed at www.drugs.com/bupropion.html.

American Cancer Society. www.cancer.org. The ACS Web site discusses the use of bupropion for smoking cessation.

Chantix.com. Pfizer's Web site devoted to Chantix has some overall useful information.

Drugs.com/chantix.html. I find drugs.com to be an excellent Web site for providing detailed information on Chantix.

– 6 –

Treatment centers

– 6 –

Treatment centers

"Until I went to rehab, I didn't understand what it did."

—*Aaron Neville*

Smoking cessation clinics or treatment centers are located all throughout the country. Some of these centers offer only outpatient services, while others also provide inpatient treatment. You'll find that many hospitals have cessation treatment clinics or centers for patients being treated for other conditions, but they all have programs to help people who want to quit smoking. The easiest way to find a treatment center is to call the American Cancer Society, American Lung Association, or the American Heart

Association. You can also call your local hospital or medical center.

You've probably never heard of using inpatient therapy to help quit smoking. When most people think of going "inpatient," they associate it with programs for alcoholics, drug addicts, or people battling psychological problems. But for smoking? They exist as another cessation option if you have the time and money.

The advantage of attending an inpatient program is receiving highly specialized care. Doctors, nurses, counselors, and others are there to help you get through the most difficult phase of quitting—the first couple of weeks. From a physical standpoint, those first weeks are the hardest as your body withdraws from the nicotine.

The easiest way to find out if there's an inpatient smoking cessation program near you is to pick up the phone and call around. Call your doctor, local hospitals, the American Cancer Society, or other health organizations. The Internet can also be a useful tool for locating inpatient programs. There are a handful of inpatient programs I know about. The Mayo Clinic offers an intensive inpatient program. The Saint Helena Center in California, the Mandala Wellness Retreat and Spa, and the Seabrook House also provide inpatient care. Finally, there is the Hazelden organization program in Minnesota.

Because these are not long-term programs, you'll have plenty of work to do once you leave. You'll return to the daily stressors in life and will most likely be tempted to light up on occasion. In my opinion, that may be the one drawback of an inpatient program—you go from a controlled environment back to a "normal" one. It's easier to refrain from smoking when you have no access to cigarettes and are in a setting designed to be supportive. Once you walk out the doors, you can easily go down the street to buy a pack. Not to mention you'll be subjected to the same stressors that you experienced before starting the program. All programs offer coping-skills training, which is an important part to long-term

smoking abstinence. Learning the skills and successfully using them are two different matters, though.

With all of that in mind, if you think any type of
treatment program (outpatient, intensive outpatient,
or inpatient) will help you, check it out.

Resources

*Note: This information does not constitute an
        endorsement of these programs.*

Hazelden Residential Tobacco Recovery Program.
www.hazelden.org/web/public/tobaccorecovery.page.
The Hazelden Foundation offers drug- and alcohol-
addiction treatment services. Their seven-day inpatient smoking cessation program is located at the
Center City, Minnesota, campus.

Mayo Clinic Nicotine Dependence Center.
www.mayoclinic.org/ndc-rst. Having lived in Roch-
ester, Minnesota, where the program is located, I

used to receive my medical care from the Mayo Clinic and can attest to the quality of their services. The telephone number for this world-renowned medical center is 800.344.5984.

Mandala Wellness Retreat and Spa. www.mandalaretreat.com. This wellness retreat and spa center, located about an hour north of Atlanta, Georgia, offers four-day and six-day retreats for smoking cessation. You can stay onsite or offsite during your visit. Based on the organization's Web site, they use a holistic approach for smoking cessation. Their telephone number is 706.878.0036.

Saint Helena Center for Health. www.smokefreelife.com. Located in California, the Center offers a seven-day smoking-cessation program. According to the Center's Web site, approximately 66 percent of people report being smoke-free a year after completing their weeklong program. Their telephone number is 800.358.9195.

Seabrook House Nicotine Addiction Recovery Rehab and Drug Treatment Detox Facility. www.seabrookhouse.org/nicotine.asp. This organization is located in New Jersey. You'll need to call 800.761.7575 to learn more information about their smoking-cessation program.

– 7 –

Psychological therapy

– 7 –

Psychological therapy

"Is your problem really your problem? Or, is your problem your attitude toward your problem?"
— *Joyce Meyer*

Cognitive behavioral therapy

If you know anything about mental health counseling, chances are you've heard about cognitive behavioral therapy (CBT). Cognitive behavioral therapy has become one of the most common methods used to treat mental health issues, such as depression and anxiety disorders. It can also be used to help accomplish other goals, such as weight loss, smoking cessation, overcoming addictions, relationship improvement, anger management, and so on.

Cognitive behavioral therapy refers to a form of therapy that focuses on the role thinking plays in both our feelings and behaviors. There is not just one technique used in CBT as it refers to a group of approaches. One premise of this approach is that you are responsible for your thoughts, moods, and behavior. This means taking responsibility for them instead of saying others have caused them. For example, if you get mad at someone, then the act of getting mad is on you—you can either choose to get mad or find another way to approach the problem that is healthier for your mind and body.

Now, you may think this is bogus. Trust me, you're not alone. Plenty of people believe what they think and how they feel is a result of other peoples' actions. Part of CBT is to help retrain your thinking; instead of automatically getting mad at someone or something, you are able to step back and take control of your emotions. You can't control what others do, but you can control how you react to others.

As it relates to smoking, CBT can help you better cope with stress. Many, if not most, smokers will smoke to deal with stress. After a while it becomes automatic. Something stresses you out, which leads you to light up so that you'll calm down. Let's look at this step-by-step for a minute.

Maybe you have just received a bad evaluation from your boss and have become worried and angry. One way you often deal with such feelings is to smoke. Using CBT you learn to control your thoughts and emotions. This isn't to say that the negative evaluation won't bother you. However, CBT techniques will help you remain calmer during stressful situations so that you can look at the event more objectively. Is the evaluation as bad as you think? Was your boss really upset or just pointing out some issues so you can improve? Remaining calm in a stressful situation will help you keep control of your emotions. Being in control of your emotions will help prevent you from smoking and allow you to look for more productive ways to deal with the situation.

According to the National Association of Cognitive-Behavioral Therapists, most CBT approaches share the following features. One feature is the view that our thoughts cause our feelings and behaviors. This is extremely important to remember—thoughts lead to feelings, which lead to behavior. When you have better control over your thoughts, you'll also have better control over your feelings and behavior.

Another aspect of CBT is its relatively short duration. This approach is not designed to go on indefinitely. According to the NACBT, a patient receives an average of sixteen sessions when dealing with any disorder. That's four months if there is one session each week.

A third critical element of CBT is homework. For the CBT approach to work, you need to put forth effort. Typically after each section, you'll be asked to complete some assignments, which will be discussed in the following session. If you go to the psychology or self-help section of your local bookstore, you'll find plenty of books on CBT (assuming they're in stock). Many will be workbooks. If you enroll in a smoking-cessation group in which the counselor uses CBT, you may receive a workbook to use. The same applies if you see a counselor on your own. Even if a workbook is not used, the counselor will give you assignments.

Dr. Kathleen Carroll of Yale University wrote a book on CBT and cocaine addiction that is in the public domain and can be found on the Web site of the National Institute of Drug Abuse. The reason I'm going to briefly discuss the book is that it focuses on CBT in helping to treat addictions. Remember, smoking is an addiction, and Dr. Carroll's information is just as relevant for this addiction.

According to Dr. Carroll, there are two key components to CBT: functional analysis and skills training. Functional analysis refers to identifying thoughts, feelings, and circumstances prior to and after a behavior. In our case, that would be before and after smoking. This analysis helps to identify triggers that lead to smoking and to figure out why smoking was the behavior of choice instead of doing something else. The analysis also helps identify the feelings associated with the event and with smoking. How did you feel before lighting up? And after?

The skills-training aspect focuses on developing healthy coping mechanisms. This means developing better control over emotions and finding healthier outlets when dealing with stress.

With all this talk on the use of therapy, chances are you are wondering if you really need it. After all, you want to quit smoking, not become some touchy-feely person who's in tune with your emotions. Well, thankfully, there's a substantial amount of research that shows why CBT is an effective smoking-cessation tool. Several studies have shown that smokers are more likely to relapse in situations that cause negative feelings such as anxiety, depression, or anger. Other research indicates that relapses could be predicted by mood. In particular, many smokers have indicated they relapsed while in a negative frame of mind.

Other studies have shown that coping strategies help reduce the urge to smoke during stressful situations. Cognitive strategies such as being optimistic and engaging in positive self-talk helped reduce smoking urges rather than just make the urges more tolerable.

A recent study used CBT in conjunction with bupropion and the nicotine patch. For the first eight weeks, all patients received CBT, and they also received the patch and medication for the first nine weeks. Following the first nine weeks, half of the patients were randomly selected to receive twelve more weeks of CBT. Furthermore, they received telephone counseling and messages from the clinic. The other half of the patients received four telephone calls during the additional twelve weeks. These calls were supportive in nature, designed to help keep people motivated, answer questions, and learn about any issues or symptoms patients were experiencing. At the end of the study, those who received CBT had better results. Forty-five percent of

CBT participants had not smoked in at least a week, while 29 percent of those receiving just the phone calls indicated they had not smoked in at least a week. Unfortunately, when the researchers followed up after one year, there was no significant difference in the number of patients who still abstained from smoking (31 percent for the CBT group, 27 percent for the other group).

Finally, if you're worried about gaining weight when you quit smoking, then CBT can help in that department too. Research has shown that CBT can help protect against weight gain for smokers who are quitting.

Aversion therapy

Are you up for eating a can of dog food? Or maybe locking yourself in a closet and smoking a couple packs of cigarettes without taking a break? Or calling up and complementing the most annoying ex-boyfriend or ex-girlfriend you've ever had?

If any of these want to make you gag, then you may want to consider aversion therapy to help you quit smoking.

The principle behind aversion therapy is simple: there is an immediate negative consequence for engaging in a behavior. You know it can feel rewarding to smoke. The goal of aversion therapy is to pair smoking with a negative consequence. As a result, smoking will no longer be associated with something good, but with something bad.

As one of the most studied ways to quit smoking, aversion therapy has received mixed support in the medical and psychological research circles. Techniques such as rapid smoking achieve short-term results, but the effect is generally not sustained over longer periods of time. Of course, as with other approaches discussed in this book, positive long-term results are always lower than short-term results. Plus, the use of nicotine replacement therapies and medications provide smokers with less painful approaches to quitting.

I'm not a fan of aversion therapy for a couple of reasons. I don't know too many people who will follow through with it. Unless you will follow through with whatever consequence is paired with smoking, it's a waste of time. Plus, people tend to get angry when they hurt. It's hard enough to quit—why become more angered or irritated during the process? Having said that, there are several methods you can try if you do want to explore aversion therapy.

Rapid smoking involves taking a puff from a cigarette every six to ten seconds. This is repeated for a set period of time, or until nausea sets in, while the person focuses on the negative sensations it causes. The process is repeated until the smoker grows sick of smoking.

One study that examined rapid smoking produced positive results. Researchers had patients engage in rapid smoking, taking a puff every six seconds and exceeding no more than nine cigarettes during the session. After the third cigarette, the participant took a five-minute break. During a different session, the participants were allowed to smoke three cigarettes at their own pace within a thirty-minute time limit. This is referred to as self-paced smoking.

After each of the sessions, the participants could not smoke at all for three hours. During this time the researchers measured the intensity of the smokers' cravings. After the rapid-smoking session, the participants had significantly lower levels of cravings compared to the other group's after their self-paced session. Furthermore, during the rapid-smoking sessions, the participants scored higher on nausea and dizziness. In fact, only one participant managed to smoke all nine cigarettes; the other participants became too nauseated. Fifty percent also vomited during the rapid-smoking session.

Self-paced smoking is really no different than plain old smoking. However, if you smoke in this manner, you should focus on the negative sensations you feel and consequences your body experiences. The more vivid the negative sensations are, the more nauseated you'll become while smoking.

Another form of aversion therapy you can try is "smoke holding." Take a big puff on a cigarette and keep the smoke in your mouth. Hold it there for thirty seconds while you continue to breathe through your nose. Be sure to focus on the taste and other sensations you feel as the smoke lingers on your teeth, gums, and tongue. This should help induce nausea.

The rubber-band technique, another form of aversion therapy, requires you to wear a rubber band around your wrist. Every time you have an urge to smoke, pull the rubber band and let it go. It'll sting your wrist and hopefully act as a deterrent. If you want to inflict more pain, put a few rubber bands on your wrist. And make sure each has enough give so you can pull back really far. Use them at the same time and watch the small welts form on your wrist. If you're dedicated to this approach, you can abandon the rubber band and buy a wooden ruler. Every time you get the urge to smoke, crack the ruler over your knuckles (I say this jokingly—splitting your knuckles open isn't something you should do).

Excessive smoking is another technique you can try. Instead of reducing how many cigarettes you smoke, you temporarily increase them. Similar to rapid smoking, the goal is to become physically ill when you smoke. However, I know of an instance in which this method unfortunately backfired. When one of my relatives was a kid, he was caught smoking. His father then bought him a box of cigars and made him go into a closet and smoke all of them. If he could finish them, his father would let him smoke. Sure enough, he managed to smoke all the cigars but was pretty ill for a while. Even though his father was surprised that his plan backfired, he allowed his son to keep smoking.

Shock therapy is another type of aversion therapy that has been tried in the past. During this therapy, participants received a shock when they puffed on a cigarette. Another puff, another shock. After so many puffs, they equated smoking with getting shocked. One study found shock therapy to be effective, although it did not involve actual smoking.

Over a course of eight sessions, participants would describe their smoking experiences and receive shocks to their index fingers. Compared to the group who did not receive the shock therapy, smokers who had received shocks were almost three times more likely to quit smoking.

In general, aversion therapy is not highly regarded. Rewarding proper behavior is considered better than punishing improper behavior. Also, there can be ethical problems with this type of therapy, such as how much punishment is too much? Techniques such as smoke holding and rapid smoking are better approaches than using shocks, rubber bands, or other methods of self-inflicting pain.

Although some people may believe this is nitpicking, I believe there is a difference between suppressing an urge and eliminating an urge. Aversion therapy is designed to suppress an urge, which will hopefully lead to eliminating the urge over time. Other methods, such as nicotine replacement therapies, medications, and cognitive behavioral therapies focus more on eliminating the urge than suppressing it. It still takes time, but doesn't involve using "punishments" along the way.

Resources

Mayo Clinic. www.mayoclinic.com. The Mayo Clinic's Web site has information on medications, cognitive behavioral therapy, and smoking.

National Association of Cognitive Behavioral Therapists. www.nacbt.org. A good resource for learning more about CBT and locating therapists in your area.

National Alliance on Mental Illness. www.nami.org. Obviously the organization's focus is on mental illnesses. However, they do have information regarding cognitive behavioral therapy, as well as material on various medications.

Change Your Thinking: Overcome Stress, Combat Anxiety and Depression, and Improve Your Life with CBT. Written by Dr. Sarah Edelman and published by Da Capo Press (2007).

Feel the Way You Want to Feel. No Matter What! Written by Dr. Aldo Pucci and published by iUniverse (2008).

Feeling Better, Getting Better, Staying Better. Written by Dr. Albert Ellis and published by Impact Publishers (2001).

Sex, Drugs, Gambling, and Chocolate. Written by Dr. A. Thomas Horvath and published by Impact Publishers (2003).

− 8 −

Combination approaches

– 8 –

Combination approaches

"Our attitude toward life determines life's attitude towards us."

—*Earl Nightingale*

You're not stuck using one option at a time to try to quit smoking. In fact, that is not recommended. You should use as many resources as possible to help overcome the addiction. The more approaches you incorporate, the greater your chances of success.

If you go back to the chapters on medications and nicotine replacement therapies, you'll see that every option increased the chances of quitting. On average, any individual approach doubles your chances of quitting. However, because quitting is so hard, why just double your chances of success? Keep increasing the odds so they're in your favor.

Combination approaches involve adding medications, nicotine replacement therapy, and psychological therapy options together. The specific combination is up to you and your doctor. Medications and NRT can be combined with a doctor's approval. The same holds true for using more than one NRT. Adding individual or group therapy to the mix will be ideal. Remember, the key to long-term success is to handle urges, cravings, and especially stress.

A study was published at the end of 2009 in which the authors conducted head-to-head trials of various medications and nicotine replacement therapies. The researchers found that using the nicotine patch with the nicotine lozenge gave patients the greatest chance of success. Zyban (bupropion) was used alone and in combination with the lozenge. Still, it did not do as well as the patch-lozenge combination. Chantix (varenicline) was not used in this study.

A review article by some doctors looked at existing research that compared the effectiveness of combination approaches versus a single approach. Their review indicated that combination approaches were consistently more effective than single approaches. In one study there was almost a 40 percent abstinence rate at the three-month mark for people who used a combination of nicotine gum and a patch. This compares to 28 percent of people who used only the nicotine gum. A similar study found that the gum and patch produced a 34 percent abstinence rate at the three-month mark, while the abstinence rate for those using only the patch was 22.7 percent. A nicotine patch and nasal spray combination also proved more effective than the patch alone.

One study found that the number of medications used was related to the chances of success. After four weeks, 82 percent of those who were taking at least four medications (NRT and/or prescription medications) were abstinent. This compares to 74 percent of people who took three medications, 64 percent who took two medications, 52 percent who took one medication, and 31 percent who were not taking any medications. However, at the six-month mark, there was not much of a difference: 42 percent of those on at least four medications were still abstinent, while 37 percent of those on one medication were abstinent.

Another study examined the effectiveness of nicotine gum and the patch together versus just the patch. The patch was used for three months, and those who were given the gum were encouraged to use it for up to six months. Predictably, those who used the patch and gum were more likely to be smoke-free at the end of one year. However, the results were still dismal in this study: after one year only 13 percent of those on the patch and gum were still abstinent. None of the people who used only the patch were still abstinent.

In one study the authors looked at four treatment methods using both single and combination approaches. The study compared CBT with the patch and without the patch, as well as exercise with and without the patch. The authors found that the combination approaches worked better than the single approaches. For example, at the end of treatment, 77 percent using the patch plus CBT had continually been abstinent. By comparison, only 59 percent of those receiving just CBT had been smoke-free since the start of the study. Similar findings occurred for the other group: 70 percent of those receiving the exercise and patch program had continually been abstinent. Only 49 percent of those in the exercise alone group had similar results.

Not all of the research finds combination approaches to be more effective than single approaches. There can be a variety of reasons for that: problems with how the study was conducted, abnormal results (compared to other studies), or a combination that was genuinely not effective. For example, one study examined the effectiveness of fluoxetine and a nicotine inhaler. Results indicated there was no added benefit of the fluoxetine when compared to those who used only the inhaler. Another study found that the combination of varenicline and the patch was no more effective than the patch alone.

Regardless of whether a study has positive or negative findings, it is important to remember that one study doesn't provide a complete picture. Several studies showing similar results provide a better idea of whether something really works.

When considering the best combination of treatments you can use, ask your doctor, tobacco-cessation program counselor, or medical professional. There is no one right combination; it will depend on your physical health, mental health, and smoking history.

– 9 –

Support groups
and quitlines

– 9 –

Support groups and quitlines

"God, grant me the serenity to accept the things I cannot change, the courage to change the things I can, and the wisdom to know the difference."
—Reinhold Niebuhr

Support Groups

There are support groups for everything: drinking, drug addiction, Internet addiction, emotional disorders, and so on. There are even support groups for smoking. Why bother with a support group? To support each other when the going gets tough.

There are two types of smoking-cessation support groups: in-person and online. If you're interested in the in-person groups, the best place to start is with your doctor. He should have information you can use, but if not, try the local hospital. When you call, tell the operator what you're looking for, and she should be able to connect you with the right person. You can also ask for community relations or patient relations. It's common for hospitals to receive these requests, so someone should be able to point you in the right direction. In case none of those options work, call the local chapter of the American Cancer Association, American Lung Association, or American Heart Association.

Nicotine Anonymous, which started in the 1980s, is a worldwide support group with chapters across several countries. The group uses a twelve-step program that has been adopted from Alcoholics Anonymous. Of course, it is possible that a local group does not exist in your area, so you can either start one yourself or go online. Nicotine Anonymous offers online support groups, "e-mail pals," and traditional pen pals. There are also telephone meetings you can attend.

Membership in the group can be ongoing because it is not a time-limited withdrawal program. Just like other support groups, people can join and stay as long as they want. Depending on where you live, there may be a steady stream of new members.

Members are encouraged to have sponsors whose job is to be a key support. Members are also encouraged to share phone numbers with each other. The more people a person can turn to in a tough time, the better.

QUITNET is an online support group billed as the "Web's Largest Quit Smoking Community." Basic membership is free and provides access to a variety of resources. A paid membership allows you to use even more features, such as forums where you can post and answer questions. A chat feature also exists so you can immediately speak with other members who are online. You can also e-mail other members and find "quit buddies."

If you find support networks to be helpful, then check around for a group near you. Just make sure you all don't go out for drinks after the meetings— chances are that won't end too well, at least in terms of staying smoke-free.

Quitlines

"I'm going to get through this; I'm going to be fine. The power to do it is all in my mind."
—Cindy Wagner

Over the past several years, the popularity of quitlines has grown. A quitline is a phone number you call to receive free help with smoking cessation. Services include phone counseling, self-help advice, and informational material. Think of a quitline as an information clearinghouse: if you have a question, the folks there can most likely answer it or tell you where to find the answer.

Quitlines are available in all fifty states, Washington, D.C., and the five U.S. territories. The national quitline will redirect you to the quitline in your state.

Quitlines offer a variety of services to people who want to stop smoking, including telephone counseling. Several types of phone counseling exist, and each state differs as to the type of counseling offered. In general, quitlines offer proactive and reactive counseling, single-session counseling, and brief-intervention counseling.

Proactive counseling is an especially nice service. Counselors from the quitline will call you to see how you're doing and check on your progress. According to a 2008 survey of quitlines published by the North American Quitline Consortium, 100 percent of quitlines in the United States offer proactive telephone counseling. They'll answer any questions, provide words of encouragement, and help you stay motivated to quit. You'll have to check with your quitline to see how often this service is offered. Each quitline has eligibility criteria you'll need to meet in order to receive proactive counseling.

The other types of phone counseling are reactive. In order to receive help and support, you need to call the quitline. Similar to proactive sessions, your state's quitline may only provide a certain number of phone sessions.

When calling the quitline for the first time, you will need to enroll in the program, which will take an estimated 15 minutes based on data provided by the NAQC. The length of the first telephone counseling session is approximately thirty minutes. States are willing to invest the time to help you quit smoking.

States are also willing to invest the money. According to the NAQC, in 2008 there were thirty-seven states that offered free nicotine patches to people. Thirty states offered free nicotine gum, while eighteen states provided nicotine lozenges. Five states offered discounted nicotine replacement therapies.

Quitlines will also mail you literature if you wish. However, it's worth noting that most quitlines have a Web site. You should be able to find the same materials there and download them straight to your computer. If you are looking for information and can't find it on the quitline's Web site, call them or send an e-mail, and they'll let you know whether they have what you want.

Resources

American Cancer Society. www.cancer.org.

American Heart Association. www.americanheart.org.

American Lung Association. www.lungusa.org.

Nicotine Anonymous. www.nicotine-anonymous.org.

QUITNET. www.quitnet.com.

National Quitline. 1.800.QUIT.NOW. http:// 1800quitnow.cancer.gov. By calling the national number, you will automatically be connected with the quitline in your state.

– 10 –

Diet and exercise

– 10 –

Diet and exercise

"Life is a succession of moments. To live each one is to succeed."

—*Corita Kent*

D iet and exercise can help in several ways. The first way is that they help provide a motivation to quit and stay smoke-free. If you make lifestyle changes to improve your health, it will give you an incentive to quit. If you only quit smoking without making diet and exercise changes, then there is less to lose if you decide to start again. If you quit smoking, start exercising, and eating better, then by smoking again you'll be compromising the benefits of eating and exercising. In a sense, you're investing more in yourself by taking a comprehensive approach to health.

Exercise is also important for those worried about weight gain. The more you exercise, the more likely your weight will either stay the same (if you start snacking a lot) or drop.

Exercise

Both short and long exercise sessions have been shown to help with withdrawal symptoms and decrease the desire to smoke. If you recall, withdrawal symptoms typically last no longer than a month, and most only last a couple of weeks. Exercising during this time will help reduce the withdrawal symptoms. Why? Part of the reason is psychological. Exercise has been shown to help improve mood and reduce both tension and stress.

If you're like many people, you don't have a lot of free time on your hands. It may be difficult to set aside an hour or so on a daily basis to exercise. However, one study demonstrated that even a twenty-minute period of exercise helped with withdrawal symptoms and decreased the desire to smoke. One interesting aspect of this study was that participants had not smoked for approximately fifteen hours prior to the exercise. Since they were current smokers, there was no active attempt to quit. Even so, exercise helped temporarily improve concentration, reduce tension, lower stress and irritability, and lessen restlessness.

Another study found that a fifteen-minute brisk walk helped reduce the urge to smoke, at least short term. If you're allowed fifteen-minute breaks at work, go for a walk when you have the time. Even though a short walk only temporarily reduces the urge to smoke, it'll help you get through your day.

Some research has examined the combination of exercise and nicotine replacement therapy. It shouldn't come as a shock that adding NRT to an exercise program increases the chances of successfully quitting. One study showed that after a six-week period, 70 percent of women had been able to refrain from smoking after starting an NRT and exercise regimen.

Two established factors that help prevent smoking relapse are high self-esteem and a strong coping ability. The better we look and feel, the more self-esteem we tend to have. Exercise helps with both of these—it makes us look better and feel more attractive by increasing muscle development and promoting weight loss.

To maintain long-lasting effects of exercise, you'll need to incorporate it into your lifestyle. If you exercise while quitting smoking and then stop exercising, the results won't be beneficial in the long run.

If you're going to quit cold turkey, then exercising will definitely benefit you. As I've mentioned a few times throughout the book, withdrawal symptoms make quitting cold turkey pretty difficult. Given what we know about the role exercise plays in reducing stress and improving mood, it will definitely help you resist the temptation to smoke.

Diet

Diet plays a role in smoking cessation for several reasons. Weight gain is a concern for many people who want to quit. Smokers tend to eat more during the quitting process. However, there's nothing about smoking withdrawal that physically makes a person eat. Having said that, nicotine does increase your metabolism, so you burn more calories a day when smoking. Your metabolism will slow down as you quit, which means you may initially gain a couple of pounds. It is typically a stress-and-distraction response. If you find that you're making more frequent trips to the fridge while quitting, consider eating healthier foods.

What you eat is important to your overall well-being. The same dietary advice you'll hear to help you quit smoking is basically the same advice you'll hear about dieting in general: drink more water, eat less junk, and choose healthier foods.

First, drink more water to help flush your system. The typical recommendation is 64 ounces of water a day. Years ago I learned about the work of Dr. Batmanghelidj, who wrote the books *Your Body's Many Cries for Water* and *Water: For Health, For Healing, For Life.* The basic premise of his work is we don't drink enough water, which leads to a lot of problems with the body. In the spring of 2002, I listened to a radio interview regarding Dr. Batmanghelidj's work. In the interview a formula was given to help people determine how much water they should drink daily. The formula was pretty simple: take your weight and divide it in half. That number is how many fluid ounces of water you should drink daily. For example, let's say you weigh 230 pounds. Dividing that in half gives us 115, so according to Dr. Batmanghelidj, you should drink 115 ounces—around 14 cups—of water to be properly hydrated.

I've always drunk more than the standard 64 ounces, and more often than not exceed the doctor's recommendation. Because of that it's hard for me to say whether the additional water intake helps. I do know that on the occasional days that I don't get enough water, I feel more worn down. If you're going to try this approach to staying properly hydrated, there's only one bit of advice you should take: ask your doctor if the amount of water you'll be drinking is too much. It is possible to drink too much water and in a way "flood" your kidneys, which can cause kidney damage.

As mentioned, it is important to eat healthier foods if you begin eating more frequently when you quit smoking. This piece of advice should still be taken even if you crave unhealthy foods. Interestingly enough, the food you eat influences the taste of cigarettes. A study that came out a few years ago reported that the food smokers ate could make cigarettes taste better or worse. Healthy foods, as you might guess, made cigarettes taste worse. This included fruits and vegetables, non-caffeinated drinks, and dairy products. Almost an equal number of smokers indicated that chocolate makes cigarettes taste better and worse. If it does make the taste worse, you may want to snack on more chocolate as a cigarette deterrent. But remember to eat chocolate in moderation—otherwise it defeats the purpose of this chapter.

The research also indicated that alcohol, meat products, and caffeinated drinks made cigarettes taste better. It's not surprising that alcohol helps the taste, given how alcohol can dull the senses. Whether this information tends to be true for you or not, it is important to limit the unhealthy foods that make cigarettes taste better and maintain a healthy balance of foods and drinks.

Supplements

There's not one magic supplement in existence that you can take to quit smoking within a couple of days. If you come across any supplements online where the company suggests this is possible, don't waste your money. If something sounds too good to be true, there's a good chance it is.

Supplements do not need to be approved by the U.S. Food and Drug Administration. This means a company does not need to provide evidence to the FDA that the supplement is safe or effective. It is up to the companies to ensure the safety of their supplements; they are not supposed to make any false or misleading claims about what the supplement can do.

This self-responsibility means that quality control can be an issue with supplements. You can look at five different brands of a supplement—all five could be either great or garbage. It's really hard to tell, and no company is going to market their product as junk. I have used supplements for over fifteen years, so the best advice I can give is to talk with a naturopath, chiropractor, or owner of a health-food store. They can usually tell you what brands to look for and which ones to avoid. The owner of a health-food store gave me one piece of advice that seems to hold true for a lot of things people buy: you get what you pay for.

There are a variety of supplements you may be able to use to help deal with possible withdrawal symptoms and mood, including kava-kava, passionflower, skullcap, catnip, hops, and St. John's wort. Valerian root, passionflower, and melatonin are believed to have sedating effects and may help with sleep. Mullein, another herb, is said to help heal damaged tissues and soothe irritated lungs.

According to several clinical studies, taking vitamins, especially vitamin C, can also benefit smokers trying to quit. This vitamin is an antioxidant, which helps protect your cells against damage. Smoking decreases vitamin C levels in the body, which makes your cells easier to damage; thus, it is important to take a vitamin C supplement. Taking vitamin A and E supplements may also be beneficial, because these vitamins are also antioxidants. A multivitamin contains all these vitamins—A, C, and E—as well as a host of others.

Be sure to let your doctor know before you start taking any supplements. Interactions can occur between supplements and medications.

Resources

American Dietetic Association. If you're looking to eat a healthier diet, this is a good place to start. The ADA Web site is www.eatright.org.

American Heart Association.
Visit www.americanheart.org for information on diet, nutrition, and exercise.

The Herbal Drugstore: The Best Natural Alternatives to Over-the-Counter and Prescription Medicines. Written by Linda B. White, M.D., and Steven Foster, published by Rodale Books (2000). A great resource for learning about herbal remedies.

Prescription for Nutritional Healing, 4th Edition. Written by Phyllis A. Balch and published by Avery Trade (2006). This is an excellent book for learning more about nutritional approaches to good health.

– 11 –

Enroll in clinical trials

– 11 –

Enroll in clinical trials

"Research is creating new knowledge."
— *Neil Armstrong*

How daring are you? If you want to be involved in some of the latest research on smoking cessation, then you should consider enrolling in available clinical trials. Clinical trials are conducted to test the safety and effectiveness of new medications and therapies. Many trials are done to compare proven therapies.

There are a few ways you can find clinical trials in your area. First, look at the advertisements in your newspaper. Often researchers will place ads to find people to participate in their trials. You may even hear radio commercials that are used to recruit participants. Another way is to contact the nearest university medical center. Research is an integral part of hospitals and medical centers.

The easiest way is to look on the Internet. All clinical trials have to be registered with the federal government, which runs a Web site called Clinical Trials.gov. You can find hundreds of clinical trials on smoking cessation or on smoking trials. You can learn about the details of the study, whether partici- pants are currently being recruited, and who you should contact. Pretty simple stuff.

There are a few things you should know when looking into clinical trials. First, not all trials are testing new medications. In fact, there are still plenty of trials evaluating the use of existing medications, such as bupropion or varenicline. For example, although bupropion's effectiveness is known, stud- ies are still comparing the success of the medication alone versus adding nicotine replacement therapies or psychological therapies, or seeing how well it works among different groups, such as young versus old smokers.

A great deal of research looks at a medication or therapy compared to a placebo medication or therapy. We know of many medications and therapies that are superior to placebos, which are sugar pills that have no impact on the body. However, we really need to learn more about how well these approaches work against each other, and among different populations (men, women, juveniles, adults, the elderly, and so forth).

If you enroll in a clinical trial where a medication is being tested, it is worth knowing you may not even receive the medication. Many trials compare medications to placebos in order to see whether the medication performs better than the placebo. One of the best ways to do this is to not let participants know whether they are getting the real or fake medication. Knowing that information may cause people to act differently, such as not taking the pill if it is the fake. Plus, if participants believe they are taking the medication, they may begin to feel better, even when they are take the placebo. This is known as the placebo effect.

You'll come across many clinical trials that are not even testing medications. Some trials are designed to compare various therapies—for example, one form of cognitive behavioral therapy versus another, CBT versus aversion therapy, or something else altogether. What you want to remember is a great deal of variety exists in clinical trials.

There are also "open label" clinical trials. If you enroll in this type of trial, you'll know what treatment you are receiving. All participants are told in advance what medication or treatment they will receive.

If you are looking for clinical trials designed to test medications, chances are you'll hear about Phase 1, Phase 2, or Phase 3 clinical trials. Phase 1 trials are designed to start learning how the medication works with people. This means seeing if the medication is safe, evaluating side effects, determining dosages, and starting to evaluate its effectiveness. A small number of participants are selected for the trial. If you enroll and are selected for a Phase 1 trial, don't be surprised if you have to stay in the hospital during the trial—doctors will want to keep a very close eye on you. This way you can be continually monitored and receive immediate help if you have a reaction to the medication. If you find a Phase 1 trial you're interested in, remember this: it takes substantial research for a new medication to even be considered for a Phase 1 trial, let alone be approved for it. The drug has to have shown promising results in laboratory tests, providing enough evidence to warrant further tests with people.

If a Phase 1 trial is successful, then a company can start a Phase 2 clinical trial. In these trials, the medication will still be evaluated for safety, this time with more participants. Researchers will collect more data to see if the medication is effective. If they believe the Phase 2 results are promising, they can move on to a Phase 3 clinical trial. These trials are much larger, enrolling hundreds or thousands of people. Based on the evidence from the Phase 1 and 2 trials, the medication appears to be safe and has worked for some patients.

Chances are you'll get paid for your participation in a clinical trial. Paying for participation is a proven way to help enroll people. Of course, there are studies participants won't get paid anything for. The one thing you should never do is pay to be in a clinical trial. If you're told you have to invest money in the project, just walk away.

Participating in clinical trials is a great way to help advance smoking cessation. At the same time, you may have to accept that you might not receive a medication and will be part of a placebo group.

Resources

ClinicalTrials.gov.

– 12 –

Natural therapy

– 12 –

Natural therapy

*"The mind commands the body and it obeys. The
mind orders itself and meets resistance."*
—Saint Augustine

Hypnosis

Hypnosis is one of the smoking cessation approaches that I classify as an alternative approach. I view alternative approaches as ways outside of mainstream medicine to deal with issues. However, this isn't to say they are better or worse than medical treatments.

Hypnosis may help you become much more relaxed, very focused, and open to suggestions. The

American Society of Clinical Hypnosis says that "hypnosis elicits and makes use of the experience of inner absorption, concentration, and focused attention. When our minds are concentrated and focused in this way, we are able to make use of the power of our minds to bring about change."

Hypnosis sometimes gets a bad rap. If you research hypnosis using the Internet, you'll come across a lot of junk. Countless companies sell products so you can hypnotize yourself and do anything and everything you've ever wanted. Although I fully believe in the power of hypnosis and the benefits it can reap, I don't buy into advertisements claiming you "can learn hypnosis in a matter of seconds and make everlasting changes in less than a minute." Those types of claims are ridiculous.

Many performers use hypnosis to make people act in weird and amusing ways. I've been to several shows where a hypnotist would hypnotize, or "put under," volunteers then make them feel like it was extremely hot—so hot that they started taking off their clothes. Or they would make them act like animals that would bark, meow, moo, or make other strange noises. And the list goes on.

The ability to make people act in embarrassing ways should highlight one point: the power of suggestion, when done properly, works wonders. And it can work for smoking cessation as well. Some hypnotists specialize in helping people with problems such as smoking.

There is no consensus as to whether hypnosis is an effective smoking-cessation method. According to the American Cancer Society, studies have not supported the notion that hypnosis works. However, a study published in 2008 did find support for hypnosis. In this study, all participants were given a two-month supply of nicotine patches, with the dosage based on the number of cigarettes they smoked daily. All participants also received three supportive phone calls during the treatment. Those who were randomly selected to receive hypnosis participated in two hypnosis training sessions. They were also given a recording they could use at home to continue practicing hypnosis. By combining hypnosis with a nicotine patch, approximately 26 percent of people were still smoke-free after six months. Only 18 percent of those in the other group had remained abstinent. After one year, 20 percent of the hypnosis group were still abstinent, while 14 percent of the other group were abstinent.

It is worth noting that for every study that produced positive results, there are studies that found no evidence of hypnosis helping with smoking cessation. There are a couple possible reasons for this. First, the quality of these studies hasn't been the greatest. Poor research means that any findings, positive or negative, will be questioned. Second, there's a chance that hypnosis is not effective, that studies concluding it is effective were simply a fluke.

I believe hypnosis has the power to help someone quit smoking. There has been a substantial amount of research done on using hypnosis to deal with short-term and chronic-pain management. Overall, the results have been very supportive: hypnosis is a useful tool for treating pain. There are even documented cases of surgeons using only hypnosis on a patient (instead of anesthesia) while performing surgery.

If hypnosis can be used to successfully help people with severe pain, why not use it to help with smoking? Quitting and staying smoke-free is a long-term process, which may be why research hasn't produced good results. Having a couple of sessions with a clinical hypnotist will not produce long-term results when it comes to treating addictions. If someone is going to use hypnosis to stop smoking, it must be on a regular basis. That doesn't mean you need to see a therapist once or twice a week for years—instead, you can practice hypnosis at home. If you do see a clinical hypnotist, that person will be able to tell you what resources to use.

In addition to working with a hypnotist, you can try self-hypnosis. Go to any bookstore or do an Internet search and you'll find plenty of resources on how to hypnotize yourself. There are plenty of CDs that provide guided imagery and hypnosis "sessions." Simply play the CD and follow the instructions. One of the benefits of this approach is you have more flexibility—you can do it any time of the day when you have some time to spare. It also doesn't cost as much as going to a hypnotist.

Hypnosis will not work for you if you're not open to the experience. If you doubt it will help you, it won't. I had a relative attend a quit-smoking hypnosis seminar. Instead of being hypnotized individually, the audience was hypnotized (it was a large, sold-out audience). The results varied dramatically. Some people felt better and did not have an urge to smoke when leaving. Other people walked outside and immediately lit up. It was as though those people were trying to prove that hypnosis didn't work. Either way, there is evidence that some people are more responsive to hypnosis than others. As with everything else discussed in this book, this method will not work for everyone.

Although side effects from hypnosis are uncommon, headache, nausea, and dizziness can occur. Most people don't experience any side effects.

Hypnosis is used to help treat a variety of medical conditions. For example, people seek hypnotists to help with nausea, pain control, reduce depression and anxiety, and lower blood pressure. It is used by respected medical doctors, so it is not a bogus form of treatment.

Meditation and visualization

"All that we are is the result of what we have thought. The mind is everything. What we think we become."—Buddha

Meditation and visualization are time-honored methods to relax, focus, and make positive changes in your life. Meditation is used to achieve a deep state of relaxation. It is similar to hypnosis; however, relaxation alone is the goal of meditation. Visualization, on the other hand, is used to bring about changes in your life. You do this by relaxing and then visualizing the changes you want to make. The goal is to make the visual as vivid as possible, incorporating sight, sound, smell, touch, and taste.

When visualizing, you need to focus as though you've already achieved the results you want. If you're just beginning your journey to quit smoking, you'll visualize as though you have already quit. Focus on what life is like being smoke-free. See yourself taking deeper breaths. Your clothes smell better. Your hair and breath smell better. You're using the additional money you have to pay off bills, buy more items you want, or save for a rainy day.

When you sleep, do you have realistic dreams, ones in which you feel awake and in the middle of all the action? That is how you want your visualizations to be. The more vivid the visualization, the more impact it will have on you.

One key to successful visualization is to incorporate positive emotions. How does the thought of being smoke-free make you feel? Happy? Proud? Relieved? Without this emotional component, the success you can achieve with visualization will be limited.

If you're going to attempt quitting by going cold turkey, then you may want to seriously consider the use of meditation and visualization. If you feel you can rely on sheer willpower to quit, then you should consider using these techniques to boost your chances of success.

Another benefit of using these techniques is they don't need to take a lot of time. If you want, you can spend half an hour or more getting into a deep state of relaxation. However, that may not always be feasible, especially when you're out or when cravings strike. There are quick meditations you can do that take only a couple of minutes and are especially useful when dealing with cravings. They will help take your mind off the craving while relaxing your body.

There are various ways to meditate. You need to be in a distraction-free environment, and you also need to be comfortable. You can also use a mantra, a word or phrase that you repeat as you relax. One of the more popular mantras is the word "Om" (which sounds like home without the "h"). Another way is to breathe deeply, focusing on the relaxing nature of your breathing. Some people will focus on each part of their body, repeatedly telling each part to relax until the whole body is relaxed. The books listed at the end of this chapter offer several different ways to relax and meditate.

Research on the effectiveness of meditation and relaxation for smoking cessation isn't great simply because there have not been many studies conducted on this topic. The research that does exist shows these practices help, however. One interesting study examined the effectiveness of guided relaxation on withdrawal symptoms and cravings for people who had stopped smoking for one night. People in the study listened to a ten-minute guided relaxation session called a "body scan" because parts of the body are focused on until the whole body is relaxed. Participants focused on their breathing and then shifted their awareness to other parts of the body. Although the session was brief, people who experienced this guided relaxation had lower levels of tension, irritability, and restlessness shortly after the experience.

Although the effects were short-lived, the results do indicate promise for such an approach. A body scan typically takes at least thirty minutes to complete. The fact that an abbreviated version was used and still produced some results is promising. It would be interesting to see whether a longer version produced better results, or whether an abbreviated version practiced at least three times a day produces a sustained or cumulative effect.

Another study examined the usefulness of meditation to help prevent drinkers from having an alcohol relapse. During the first eight weeks, people attended a weekly two-hour meditation class. They were also asked to practice at home six days a week for thirty minutes each day. After eight weeks, the participants could still meditate at home. After the first four weeks of practice, the following symptoms dropped: depression and anxiety, cravings, and overall stress. For the remainder of the study (a total of sixteen weeks), the symptoms remained relatively stable, even though the amount of time engaging in meditation decreased. At the end of sixteen weeks, more than half of the participants were still meditating at least four days a week. Overall, the results were very positive. If similar studies are ever conducted for people who want to stop smoking, I'm confident the results would also be positive.

There are no downsides to using meditation and visualization. They are beneficial in general and can be used in all parts of life. Aside from the time you may invest, there is nothing to lose by trying these practices to help you quit smoking.

Acupuncture

"Miracles happen every day. Not just in remote country villages or at holy sites halfway across the globe, but here, in our own lives." —Deepak Chopra

If you don't mind having tiny pin needles sticking out of you, then you may want to try acupuncture. According to the National Center for Complementary and Alternative Medicine, acupuncture "describes a family of procedures involving the stimulation of anatomical points on the body using a variety of techniques." The techniques can include inserting needles that can then be manipulated manually or with electricity. The Center states that approximately 3.1 million adults and 150,000 children used acupuncture in 2007.

The idea behind acupuncture is that energy blocks exist in the body, causing physical and emotional problems. By removing the blocks and getting the energy to flow properly, problems are reduced or disappear. The needles used to help remove the blocks are extremely thin and nothing like those used to draw blood. Acupuncturists can use different types of needles that vary in size. Luckily, none of the needles are as crude as the ones used centuries ago—those were made out of bamboo, bones, and stone. Even worse, they were a bit wider, so people definitely felt when the needles were inserted.

You typically don't have to worry about side effects from acupuncture. The spots where the needles entered may be sore for a little while. You also don't have to worry about infections as long as the needles are sterile. Many acupuncturists use disposable needles; they're used once and thrown away. If the doctor you see does not use these needles, you should at least ask how the needles are sterilized. If unsterile needles are used, then you could develop infections.

I've tried acupuncture and never had a problem with it. There is a slight sting when the needles go in, but that disappears quickly. I had a little soreness in those areas later during the day.

Acupuncture is valued in the medical field. There are currently over 200 trials underway using acupuncture for a variety of conditions. Acupuncture is being studied for chronic constipation, infant colic, healing of surgical wounds, and spinal cord injuries.

It has been shown to be beneficial for conditions such as pain syndromes, psychological illnesses, and addictions. However, the scientific evidence of acupuncture's effectiveness is mixed. Depending on what literature you read, studies have shown that it either helps or doesn't help for smoking cessation. The American Cancer Society says there is not sufficient evidence to say that acupuncture is an effective cessation tool.

A study published back in 2001 looked at the effectiveness of acupuncture on smoking cessation. This study was unique because it had a five-year follow-up period. Treatment consisted of receiving acupuncture twice a week for three weeks. Participants were instructed to use acupressure on certain parts of the ear then practice it four times a day. The control group also received acupuncture, but it was applied to locations believed to be unrelated to smoking.

Prior to the acupuncture, people smoked an average of nineteen cigarettes a day. People who received the true acupuncture dropped the number of cigarettes they smoked daily to an average of five. That's a 75 percent decrease! Those who received the fake acupuncture dropped to smoking an average of eight cigarettes a day (a 39 percent decrease). Eight months later, people in both groups had increased the number of cigarettes they smoked, but the average was still lower than the original nineteen per day. More than 20 percent of people who received the acupuncture were no longer smoking. Five years later, 18 percent were still not smoking.

A more recent study, published in 2007, reported on the effectivity of laser acupuncture and smoking cessation among three groups of people. In laser acupuncture, instead of using needles, a therapist uses a low-energy laser beam to stimulate acupuncture points. The first group received three real treatments and a fourth false treatment. The second group received four real treatments, while the third group received all false treatments.

Only 14 percent of those who received the fake treatments stopped smoking at the end of the treatment. However, 41 percent of those who received three real acupuncture treatments had stopped smoking, while 75 percent of those who received four real treatments had also stopped. Six months later, 6 percent of those in the fake treatment group were still abstinent. This compares to 19 percent for people receiving three real treatments and 55 percent for those receiving four real treatments.

Those are some impressive findings. Additional studies will need to be conducted and published to see whether similar results occur. But if these findings hold, then the effectiveness of this type of treatment rivals that of nicotine replacement therapies and medications. Furthermore, if these laser acupuncture treatments are used over a longer period of time, the results may prove to be even higher. Pharmaceutical companies may not be too thrilled with a treatment that could replace medications, but it would be good news for the rest of us!

Resources

American Society of Clinical Hypnosis.
www.asch.net. This is a professional organization
for both medical and mental health professionals
who use hypnosis in their practices. It has quality
information written for the general public on the use
of hypnosis. There is also a referral section where
you can search for practitioners in your area.

Hypnosis For Beginners. Written by William W.
Hewitt and published by Llewellyn Publications
(2002).

Self-Change Hypnosis. Written by Richard MacKen-
zie and published by Trafford Publishing (2005).

Smoke-Free Paraliminal. Produced by Learning
Strategies Corporation in Minnetonka, Minnesota.
The company produces a series of "self-improve-
ment" CDs that use a combination of music and

words to help you get into a state of relaxation and focus. Positive comments and suggestions are used to help you achieve your goal—to stop smoking. I own several products by this company and have no reservations recommending anything they sell. I even used one of their books when I taught college classes. (Unfortunately, the company probably doesn't know I exist, so I don't receive any commission!)

8 Minute Meditation: Quiet Your Mind. Change Your Life. Written by Victor Davich and published by Perigee Trade (2004).

Breath by Breath: The Liberating Practice of Insight Meditation. Written by Larry Rosenberg and published by Shambhala (2004).

Creative Visualization: Use the Power of Your Imagination to Create What You Want in Your Life. Written by Shakti Gawain and published by New World Library (2008).

Guided Meditations for Stress Reduction. Audio CD created by Bodhipaksa and sold by Wildmind Meditation Services (2004).

Meditation for Beginners. Written by Jack Kornfield and published by Sounds True (2008).

American Association of Acupuncture and Oriental Medicine. The professional association for those who practice acupuncture. The Web site (www. aaaomonline.org) has consumer information on acupuncture and lets people locate acupuncturists in their area.

Appendix

Appendix

"The man who can drive himself further once the effort gets painful is the man who will win."
— *Roger Bannister*

Incentive programs

If you're going to take the journey to quit smoking, why not try and reap some rewards along the way? I know, the best reward is improving your health and adding years to your life. Not to mention saving money, smelling better, and looking better.

What I'm talking about is earning some goodies as you quit smoking and improve your health. Many insurance companies and employers offer incentives for smoking cessation. It's cheaper for health insurance companies to help their members quit smoking than to pay for smoking-related illnesses. The savings are also passed on to employers because fewer health insurance claims mean the insurance companies don't increase the premiums as much. Healthier employees means more affordable health insurance.

The Kaiser Family Foundation and Health Research & Education Trust have collected yearly data on health insurance costs. The average annual premium for family coverage was $5,791 back in 1999. Employers paid approximately 73 percent of the premium, while employees covered the rest. In 2009 the average annual premium for family coverage was $13,375—that's an increase of 131 percent! Employers now pay closer to 74 percent of the premium, while employees cover the rest.

I'm sharing this information with you for one reason: to show that most employers have a stake in your health. The more you and your coworkers need to use your health insurance, the more the annual premiums will rise. A lot of factors are used when an insurance company decides to up the annual premium. An important factor is whether the people use the insurance. Think of it being similar to car insurance: if you don't get tickets and avoid accidents, your premium will remain relatively stable. If you get into an accident and need to file an insurance claim, your premium will jump. Get a ticket that tacks on points against your license, and your premium will go up. For employers, the same concept applies. If employees don't use the health insurance, then there won't be as high of an increase the following year. If employees need to use their health insurance, then that will factor into determining the next year's premiums.

Research has repeatedly shown that smokers have more health issues than nonsmokers. Further, work productivity is consistently lower for employees who smoke compared to those who don't smoke. Compared to nonsmokers, smokers miss more days of work each year and spend more time taking breaks throughout the day. One study found that coworkers and supervisors consistently ranked nonsmokers ahead of smokers when it came to productivity. Employers, if for no other reason, have a financial incentive to reduce the number of employees who smoke. So ask a person from human resources if employer-sponsored incentive programs are available. If there isn't one, suggest starting one.

A study examined an incentive program used across several U.S. worksites of an international company. Employees who smoked were randomly selected to receive either information about smoking cessation programs or information about the programs and accompanying financial incentives. Employees who completed a local smoking cessation program would receive $100. Employees who quit smoking within six months received another $250. If these employees managed to stay smoke-free for another six months, they would receive an additional $400. This means that if a person successfully quit smoking for the long haul, a total of $750 could be made.

The results confirmed that incentive programs have more appeal and do work. Slightly more than 5 percent of the people who only received information on local cessation programs enrolled in one. Almost three times as many people enrolled in a program if they also received the financial incentive materials.

The best way to find out whether there are any incentive programs to enroll in is to simply ask around. Talk to the person at work in charge of health insurance benefits. Call your health insurance provider and see what health and wellness programs they have. Your health insurance company will be glad to point you in the right direction.

Things to remember

"Success seems to be connected with action. Successful people keep moving. They make mistakes, but they don't quit." —Conrad Hilton

Several solutions, techniques, and therapies have been discussed in this book that you can use to help you stop smoking. Everything mentioned has been shown to work, whether for many people or very few people. However, as I'm sure you have noticed, the success rate for any particular practice isn't that high. And the success rates drop the longer someone participates in a particular treatment.

Depending on your perspective, you may think nothing works too well. Hopefully that isn't the case. Smoking is a very addictive habit and is probably a big part of your life. You can remove the nicotine and other chemicals from your system and be physically free of the addiction, but unfortunately, there is a huge psychological element to addiction that is more difficult to control. However, it is not impossible to overcome.

There are a few things I'd like you to remember as you progress in your efforts to stop smoking. First, don't give up. It doesn't matter if you need two, three, four, or more attempts to quit. Keep working at it and you'll get there. Having said that, work smartly. If something doesn't work for you, step back and evaluate what's going on. Maybe you need to add or change a medication, use a nicotine replacement therapy, or find someone else to help you. Whatever is going on, be sure to evaluate your progress as you go along. If something is not working, try something else. There's no reason to keep going down the same path if it isn't leading you anywhere productive.

Try not to give in to peer pressure if you have friends or family who still smoke. The "one-cigarette-won't-hurt" attitude will hurt at some point. I know someone who had stopped smoking for twenty years. Then she had a cigarette one day and now she's spent the better part of a year trying to quit again.

If you hear or see advertisements for "miracle" cures, be skeptical before buying anything. There's no such thing as a miracle cure for smoking cessation. No one has discovered a real instant cure, unless you count going cold turkey. If you see something you'd like to try, don't be too upset if it doesn't work, or if that "money-back guarantee" proves to be bogus. Unfortunately, there are many people who like to take advantage of others' problems and addictions.

There are plenty of resources available to you. The American Cancer Society, American Heart Association, American Lung Association, state quitlines, hospitals, doctors, and others are there to help support you. Take advantage of everything available to you. It'll make your journey that much easier.

Good luck to you!

References

References

Chapter 2: What you're getting into

Perkins, Kenneth A., Jessica Briski, Carolyn Fonte, John Scott, and Caryn Lerman. 2009. Severity of tobacco abstinence symptoms varies by time of day. *Nicotine & Tobacco Research* 11:84-91.

Chapter 3: Quitting cold turkey

Cheong, Yooseock, Hua-Hie Yong, and Ron Borland. 2007. Does how you quit affect success? A comparison between abrupt and gradual methods using data from the International Tobacco Control Policy Evaluation Study. *Nicotine & Tobacco Research* 9:801-810.

Chapter 4: Nicotine replacement therapy

Atzori, Giuseppe, Charlotte A. Lemmonds, Mitchell L. Kotler, Michael J. Durcan, and Julia Boyle. 2008. Efficacy of a nicotine (4 mg)-containing lozenge on the cognitive impairment of nicotine withdrawal. *Journal of Clinical Psychopharmacology* 28:667-674.

Bohadana, Abraham, Fredrik Nilsson, Thomas Rasmussen, and Yves Martinet. 2000. Nicotine inhaler and nicotine patch as a combination therapy for smoking cessation. *Archives of Internal Medicine* 160:3128-3134.

Etter, Jean-Francois. 2009. Dependence on the nicotine gum in former smokers. *Addictive Behaviors* 34:246-251.

Hajek, Peter, Robert West, Jonathan Foulds, Fredrik Nilsson, Sylvia Burrows, and Anna Meadow. 1999. Randomized comparative trial of nicotine polacrilex, a transdermal patch, nasal spray, and an inhaler. *Archives of Internal Medicine* 159:2033-2038.

Piper, Megan E., Stevens S. Smith, Tanya R. Schlam, Michael C. Fiore, Douglas E. Jorenby, David Fraser, and Timothy B. Baker. 2009. A randomized placebo-controlled clinical trial of 5 smoking cessation pharmacotherapies. *Archives of General Psychiatry* 66:1253-1262.

Schneider, Nina G., Richard Olmstead, Fredrik Nilsson, Freny Vaghaiwalla Mody, Mikael Franzon, and Kim Doan. 1996. Efficacy of a nicotine inhaler in smoking cessation: a double-blind, placebo-controlled trial. *Addiction* 91:1293-1306.

Shiffman, Saul and Stuart G. Ferguson. 2008. Nicotine patch therapy prior to quitting smoking: A meta-analysis. *Addiction* 103:557-563.

Shiffman, Saul, Stuart G. Ferguson, and Kenneth R. Strahs. 2009. Quitting by gradual smoking reduction using nicotine gum. *American Journal of Preventative Medicine* 36:96-104.

Chapter 5: Prescription medications

Ahmadi, Jamshid, Hamid Ashkani, Mojtaba Ahmadi, and Nahid Ahmadi. 2003. Twenty-four week maintenance treatment of cigarette smoking with nicotine gum, clonidine and naltrexone. *Journal of Substance Abuse Treatment* 24:251-255.

Buchhalter, August R., Reginald V. Fant, and Jack E. Henningfield. 2008. Novel pharmacological approaches for treating tobacco dependence and withdrawal. *Drugs* 68:1067-1088.

da Costa, Celia Lidia, Riad Naim Younes, and Maria Teresa Crus Lourenco. 2002. A prospective, randomized, double-blind study comparing nortriptyline to placebo. *Chest* 122:403-408.

Glassman, Alexander H., Lirio S. Covey, Gregory W. Dalack, Fay Stetner, Sarah K. Rivelli, Joseph Fleiss, and Thomas B. Cooper. 1993. Smoking cessation, clonidine, and vulnerability to nicotine among dependent smokers. *Clinical Trials and Therapeutics* 54:670-679.

Gonzales, David, Stephen I. Rennard, Mitchell Nides, Cheryl Oncken, Salomon Azoulay, Clare B. Billing, Eric J. Watsky, Jason Gong, Kathryn E. Williams, and Karen R. Reeves. 2006. Varenicline, an alpha4ß2 nicotine acetylcholine receptor partial agonist, vs. sustained-release bupropion and placebo for smoking cessation. *Journal of the American Medical Association* 296:47-55.

Hall, Sharon M., Victor I. Reus, Ricardo F. Munoz, Karen L. Sees, Gary Humfleet, Diane T. Hartz, Sydney Frederick, and Elisa Triffleman. 1998. Nortriptyline and cognitive-behavioral therapy in the treatment of cigarette smoking. *Archives of General Psychiatry* 55:683-690.

Halperin, Abigail C., Timothy A. McAfee, Lisa M. Jack, Sheryl L. Catz, Jennifer B. McClure, T. Mona Deprey, Julie Richards, Susan M. Zbikowski, and Gary E. Swan. 2009. Impact of symptoms experienced by varenicline users on tobacco treatment in a real world setting. *Journal of Substance Abuse Treatment* 36:428-434.

Hays, J. Taylor, Richard D. Hurt, Nancy A. Rigotti, Raymond Niaura, David Gonzales, Michael J. Durcan, David P. L. Sachs, Troy D. Wolter, A. Sonia Bulst, J. Andrew Johnston, and Jonathan D. White. 2001. Sustained-release bupropion for pharmacologic relapse prevention after smoking cessation. *Annals of Internal Medicine* 135:423-433.

Jorenby, Douglas E., Scott J. Leischow, Mitchell A. Nides, Stephen I. Rennard, J. Andrew Johnston, Arlene R. Hughes, Stevens S. Smith, Myra L. Muramoto, David M. Daughton, Kimberli Doan, Michael C. Fiore, and Timothy B. Baker. 1999. A controlled trial of sustained-release bupropion, a nicotine patch, or both for smoking cessation. *New England Journal of Medicine* 340:685-691.

Jorenby, Douglas E., L. Taylor Hays, Nancy A. Rigotti, Salomon Azoulay, Eric J. Watsky, Kathryn E. Williams, Clare B. Billing, Jason Gong, and Karen R. Reeves. 2006. Efficacy of varenicline, an alpha4ß2 nicotinic acetylcholine receptor partial agonist, vs. placebo or sustained release bupropion for smoking cessation. *Journal of the American Medical Association* 296:56-63.

Nides, Mitchell, Cheryl Oncken, David Gonzales, Stephen Rennard, Eric J. Watsky, Rich Anziano, and Karen R. Reeves. 2006. Smoking cessation with varenicline, a selective alpha4ß2 nicotinic receptor partial agonist. *Archives of Internal Medicine* 166:1561-1568.

Saules, Karen K., Leslie M. Schuh, Cynthia L. Arfken, Karen Reed, M. Marlyne Kilbey, and Charles R. Schuster. 2004. Double-blind placebo-controlled trial of fluoxetine in smoking cessation treatment including nicotine patch and cognitive-behavioral group therapy. *The American Journal of Addictions* 13:438-446.

Sood, Amit, Jon O. Ebbert, Darrell R. Schroeder, Ivana T. Croghan, Richa Sood, Mark W. Vander Weg, Gilbert Y. Wong, and J. Taylor Hays. 2007. Gabapentin for smoking cessation: A preliminary investigation of efficacy. *Nicotine & Tobacco Research* 9:291-298.

Spring, Bonnie, Neal Doran, Sherry Pagoto, Dennis McChargue, Jessica Werth Cook, Katherine Bailey, John Crayton, and Donald Hedeker. 2007. Fluoxetine, smoking, and history of major depression: A randomized controlled trial. *Journal of Consulting and Clinical Psychology* 75:85-94.

Tonstad, Serena, Philip Tonnesen, Peter Hajek, Kathryn E. Williams, Clare B. Billing, and Karen R. Reeves. 2006. Effect of maintenance therapy with varenicline on smoking cessation. *Journal of the American Medical Association* 296:64-71.

Williams, Kathryn E., Karen R. Reeves, Clare B. Billing, Ann M. Pennington, and Jason Gong. 2007. A double-blind study evaluating the long-term safety of varenicline for smoking cessation. *Current Medical Research and Opinions* 23:793-801.

Berecz, J. M. 1979. Maintenance of nonsmoking behavior through self-administered wrist-band aversion therapy. *Behavior Therapy* 10:669-675.

Brown, Richard A., Christopher W. Kahler, Raymond Niaura, David B. Abrams, Suzanne D. Sales, Susan E. Ramsey, Michael G. Goldstein, Ellen S. Burgess, and Ivan W. Miller. 2001. Cognitive-behavioral treatment for depression in smoking cessation. *Journal of Consulting and Clinical Psychology* 69:471-480.

Carmody, Timothy P., Cassandra Vieten, and John A. Astin. 2007. Negative affect, emotional acceptance, and smoking cessation. *Journal of Psychoactive Drugs* 39:499-508.

Carroll, Kathleen M. 1998. A cognitive-behavioral approach: Treating cocaine addiction. In *Therapy Manuals for Drug Addiction*. Rockville, MD: National Institutes of Health. http://www.drugabuse.gov/txmanuals/cbt/cbt1.html/.

Conway, J. B. 1977. Behavioral self-control of smoking through aversive conditioning and self-management. *Journal of Consulting and Clinical Psychology* 45:348-357.

Houtsmuller, Elisabeth J., and Maxine L. Stitzer. 1999. Manipulation of cigarette craving through rapid smoking: Efficacy and effects on smoking behavior. *Psychopharmacology* 142:149-157.

Killen, Joel D., Stephen P. Fortmann, Alan F. Schatzberg, Christina Arredondo, Greer Murphy, Chris Hayward, Maria Celio, Deann Cromp, Dalea Fong, and Maya Pandurangi. 2008. Extended cognitive behavior therapy for cigarette smoking cessation. *Addiction* 103:1381-1390.

O'Connell, Kathleen A., Vanessa L. Hosein, Joseph E. Schwartz, and Ruth Q. Leibowitz. 2007. How does coping help people resist lapses during smoking cessation? *Health Psychology* 26:77-84.

Sallit, Jennifer, Michele Ciccazzo, and Zisca Dixon. 2009. A cognitive-behavioral weight control program improves eating and smoking behaviors in weight-concerned female smokers. *Journal of the American Dietetic Association* 109:1398-1405.

Whitman, T. L. 1969. Modification of chronic smoking behavior: A comparison of three approaches. *Behaviour Research and Therapy* 7:257-263.

Chapter 8: Combination approaches

Blondal, Thorsteinn, Larus J. Gudmundsson, Kristinn Tomasson, Dagmar Jonsdottir, Holmfridur Hilmarsdottir, Fjalar Kristjansson, Fredrik Nilsson, and Unnur Steina Bjornsdottir. 1999. The effects of fluoxetine combined with nicotine inhalers in smoking cessation-a randomized trial. *Addiction* 94:1007-1015.

Cooney, Ned L., Judith L. Cooney, Bridget L. Perry, Michael Carbone, Emily H. Cohen, Howard R. Steinberg, David T. Pilkey, Kevin Sevarino, Cheryl A. Oncken, and Mark D. Litt. 2009. Smoking cessation during alcohol treatment: A randomized trial of combination nicotine patch plus nicotine gum. *Addiction* 104:1588-1596.

Ebbert, Jon O., Michael V. Burke, J. Taylor Hays, and Richard D. Hurt. 2009. Combination treatment with varenicline and nicotine replacement therapy. *Nicotine & Tobacco Research* 11:572-576.

Kornitzer, M., M. Boutsen, M. Dramaix, J. Thijs, and G. Gustavsson. 1995. Combined use of nicotine patch and gum in smoking cessation: A placebo-controlled clinical trial. *Preventive Medicine* 24:41-47.

Piper, Megan E., Stevens S. Smith, Tanya R. Schlam, Michael C. Fiore, Douglas E. Jorenby, David Fraser, and Timothy B. Baker. 2009. A randomized placebo-controlled clinical trial of 5 smoking cessation pharmacotherapies. *Archives of General Psychiatry* 66:1253-1262.

Prapavessis, Harry, Linda Cameron, J. Chris Baldi, Stewart Robinson, Kendra Borrie, Therese Harper, and J. Robert Grove. 2007. The effects of exercise and nicotine replacement therapy on smoking rates in women. *Addictive Behaviors* 32:1416-1432.

Puska, Pekka, Heikki J. Korhonen; Erkki Vartiainen, Eeva
Liisa Urjanheimo, Gunnar Gustavsson, and Ake Westin.
1995. Combined use of nicotine patch and gum compared
with gum alone in smoking cessation: A clinical trial in
North Karelia. *Tobacco Control* 4:231-235.

Shah, Sima D., Lori A. Wilken, Susan R. Winkler, and Swu-
Jane Lin. 2008. Systematic review and meta-analysis of
combination therapy for smoking cessation. *Journal of
the American Pharmacists Association* 48:659-665.

Steinberg, Michael, Jonathan Foulds, Donna L. Richardson,
Michael V. Burke, and Pooja Shah. 2006. Pharmacothera-
py and smoking cessation at a tobacco dependence clinic.
Preventive Medicine 42:114-119.

Chapter 10: Diet and exercise

McClernon, F. Joseph, Eric C. Westman, Jed E. Rose, and
Avery M. Lutz. 2007. The effects of foods, beverages,
and other factors on cigarette palatability. *Nicotine &
Tobacco Research* 9:505-510.

Prapavessis, Harry, Linda Cameron, J. Chris Baldi, Stewart
Robinson, Kendra Borrie, Therese Harper, and J. Robert
Grove. 2007. The effects of exercise and nicotine replace-
ment therapy on smoking rates in women. *Addictive
Behaviors* 32:1416-1432.

Ussher, Michael, Paola Nunziata, Mark Cropley, and Robert West. 2001. Effect of a short bout of exercise on tobacco withdrawal symptoms and desire to smoke. *Psychopharmacology* 158:66-72.

Van Rensburg, Kate Janse, and Adrian H. Taylor. 2008. The effects of acute exercise on cognitive functioning and cigarette cravings during temporary abstinence from smoking. *Human Psychopharmacology* 23:193-199.

Chapter 12: Natural therapy

Carmody, Timothy P., Carol Duncan, Joel A. Simon, Sharon Solkowitz, Joy Huggins, Sharon Lee, and Kevin Delucchi. 2008. Hypnosis for smoking cessation: A randomized trial. *Nicotine & Tobacco Research* 10:811-818.

Cropley, Mark, Michael Ussher, and Elli Charitou. 2007. Acute effects of a guided relaxation routine (body scan) on tobacco withdrawal symptoms and cravings in abstinent smokers. *Addiction* 102:989-993.

He, Dong, Jon I. Medbo, and Arne T. Hostmark. 2001. Effect of acupuncture on smoking cessation or reduction: An 8-month and 5-year follow-up study. *Preventive Medicine* 33:364-372.

Kerr, Catherine M., Paul B. Lowe, and Neil I. Spielholz. 2008. Low level laser for the stimulation of acupoints for smoking cessation: a double blind, placebo controlled randomized trial and semi structured interviews. *Journal of Chinese Medicine* 86:46-51.

Zgierska, Aleksandra, David Rabago, Megan Zuelsdorff, Christopher Coe, Michael Miller, and Michael Fleming. 2008. Mindfulness meditation for alcohol relapse prevention: A feasibility pilot study. *Journal of Addiction Medicine* 2:165-173.

Appendix

Volpp, Kevin G., Andrea B. Troxel, Mark V. Pauly, Henry A. Glick, Andrea Puig, David A. Asch, Robert Galvin, Jingsan Zhu, Fei Wan, Jill DeGuzman, Elizabeth Corbett, Janet Weiner, and Janet Audrain-McGovern. 2009. A randomized controlled trial of financial incentives for smoking cessation. *The New England Journal of Medicine* 360:699-709.

Check out these other books in the Good Things To Know series:

5 Things to Know for Successful and Lasting Weight Loss
(ISBN: 9781596525580, $9.99)

21 Things To Create a Better Life
(ISBN: 9781596525269, $9.99)

27 Things To Feng Shui Your Home
(ISBN: 9781596525672, $9.99)

29 Things To Know About Catholicism
(ISBN: 9781596525887, $9.99)

33 Things To Know About Raising Creative Kids
(ISBN: 9781596525627, $9.99)

35 Things Your Teen Won't Tell You, So I Will
(ISBN: 9781596525542, $9.99)

41 Things To Know About Autism
(ISBN: 9781596525832, $9.99)

51 Things You Should Know Before Getting Engaged
(ISBN: 9781596525481, $9.99)

99 Things to Save Money in Your Household Budget
(ISBN: 9781596525474, $9.99)

Contact Turner Publishing at (615) 255-2665
or visit turnerpublishing.com
to get your copies today!

Printed in the USA
CPSIA information can be obtained
at www.ICGtesting.com
JSHW052017140824
68134JS00027B/2511